the
pilipinx
radical imagination
reader

BOOK COVER ARTWORK BY
TRINIDAD ESCOBAR

The spiritual and theoretical positioning of this book was quite important to me. I utilized triangles as sacred shapes that absorb and transmit power. The upward triangle contains the cosmos and symbolizes the energy that we send to it. The downward triangle contains the earth and its water; this symbolizes the energy that we draw from the heavens and return to each other (as well as the land itself). It is my belief that the transmission of knowledge isn't simply a series of synapses and chemical reactions within our bodies, but that knowledge itself is consciousness—alive and eager to see itself flourish. Therefore, so long as our imaginations are boundless, our ability to learn and teach each other is boundless. The type mimics the multifaceted nature of crystals. Like the inherent shape of crystals (what many indigenous cultures see as the conscious manifestation of the earth) our own identities, experiences, and imaginations as Pilipinxs are multifaceted, reflecting and breaking apart light simultaneously. The colors found in the type are the colors of the Philippine flag but shifted. The color of peace and the color of war are, here, more representative of the new feminine era: wholeness instead of a world limited to binaries, wisdom over mere intelligence, compassion--instead of oppression—as the ultimate power.

THE
PILIPINX
RADICAL IMAGINATION
READER

edited by
Melissa-Ann Nievera-Lozano
Anthony Abulencia Santa Ana

Philippine American Writers and Artists, Inc.
San Francisco, CA

ISBN: 978-0-9981792-2-3
Library of Congress Control Number: 2018939190

Cover artwork: Trinidad Escobar
Book design: Edwin Lozada

Published by
Philippine American Writers and Artists, Inc.
P.O. Box 31928
San Francisco, CA 94131-0928

447 Sutter Street, Suite #505
San Francisco, CA 94108

pawa@pawainc.com
www.pawainc.com
pilipinxreader.com

Printed in the United States of America.

First Printing: March 2018
Second Printing: September 2018

This book is dedicated to

Filipina "Pinay" Nielo Pascasio
(11.11.1994 - 7.2.2015)

Your immense and infinite light guides us.

ACKNOWLEDGEMENTS

This project has been a huge labor of love and we want to thank the heartbeat of folx that continually supported and deeply believed in its conception. Yunnie, for creating the video, helping us manage the project, and embodying that beam of light that reminded us of the beauty and purpose of it all. Trini, for your submission, infographic and the creation of the beautiful front and back cover; so blessed that your spirit is embedded throughout the book. Dennis, for reading the submissions & providing feedback and allowing space for both Melissa and myself to journey through this process. Hiroko, for reading the submissions & providing feedback and especially taking care of Dante and Mateo while we were hard at work putting it all together. Dante and Mateo, for reminding us of the innocence, purity, playfulness, joy, and love that this book project needed in our pauses and life happenings. Edwin and PAWA, for believing in the vision of this project and making this book a reality. The contributors, who entrusted us with pieces of their soul and spirit for folx to catch a glimpse of the complexities of our diasporic community. Lastly, our ancestors and future new births that watched over us during this process so we can honor our existence in this written form. Thank you ALL from the bottom of hearts and the depths of our soul as this book is for all of us, about all of us, and by all of us.

In community solidarity,
Anthony Abulencia Santa Ana

TABLE OF CONTENTS

CUTTING OUT A SPACE: DIASPORA & MEMORY

TO BREATHE: HEALTH & WELL BEING

SUTURING OUR SPLIT SELVES: ON INTERSECTIONALITY

CAUSE A STIR: COALITIONAL CONSCIOUSNESS & ORGANIZING

HOW TO MAKE HOME: FAMILY & RADICAL PARENTING

INTRODUCTION

Who We Be

As Pilipina/o/xs[1], we continue to reclaim different parts of ourselves. It comes from our shared experiences as colonized bodies grappling with modernity and making sense of our his/herstories. When approached by Tony in the summer of 2014 with the idea of a collaborative book project, I didn't hesitate. It was a timely endeavor, to anthologize the many voices shifting the dialogue in our multifaceted community. At the time, I was moving towards finishing my dissertation exploring Pinay scholarship, while raising an infant and a toddler. Tony had returned from teaching English in Japan for some years, and was in the early stages of his own doctorate program in education where he was introduced to the work of Robin D. G. Kelley, author of *Freedom Dreams: The Black Radical Imagination* (2003). The title itself inspired him to ask: "What is our radical imagination?" We credit Dr. Kelley and countless black thinkers, cultural leaders and artists, who continue to generate language and modes of expression for communities of people of color to name and understand their own historical context in the U.S. After all, it is black culture that in some way bonded us together.

We happened to meet four years prior at a national conference, and connected as Pin@ys[2] who came of age during the "cultural renaissance"

---

[1] The F and P (for the term *Filipino/Pilipino*) are interchangeable, employed by each writer or artist according to their own context. A recent movement during academic school year of 2015-2016 called for the use of the x – as in, Pinxy, Filipinx or Pilipinx – to be inclusive of people who identify as transgender, genderqueer or non-binary. Stretching this to a/o/x (as in Piplina/o/x) expresses a sort of bridging of these multiple and inclusive gender expressions.

[2] Pin@y was a term first created to make the geopolitical distinction between Filipina/ os in the U.S. and their counterparts in the Philippines, though now used to refer to Filipina/os throughout the diaspora. The @ symbol came about in the 90s on college campuses to denote gender neutrality. I use the terms Pin@y, Filipina/o American and Filipino American interchangeably.

of the 90s. The 90s was an era in which Filipinx children of immigrant parents particularly in urban areas throughout the U.S. witnessed, practiced, and embodied forms of black culture—hip hop, graffiti, dance, and spoken word—as tools to express their own processes of ethnic identity formation. For us, it was a time when young Pinays (like me having grown up in Southeast San Diego) and Pinoys (like Tony having grown up in the San Francisco Bay Area), explored shades of resistance modeled by black thinkers, writers, educators, and artists who were most visibly on the front lines of resisting systemic oppression. Talking back, speaking up, and pushing against the status quo our parents had so easily internalized through their own colonial education in the Philippines was a contentious deed for which we were vilified or even ignored. Tired of the pressure of skin lightening, marrying up, and chasing the "American Dream," we found a language that embraced our brown-ness modeled in black culture. So this book project is a nod to the ways in which black radical thought has opened up Filipinx radical thought in these times.

Where Our Hearts Lie

As youngsters in the 90s, we saw a fight for Filipinotowns, for visibility against the backdrop of a black and white paradigm. Through our college years, the early 2000s birthed a war focused on "terror", the great recession, and exacerbating income inequality. Taking on graduate school as we approached the 2010s, we celebrated the first black president, saw the overturning of DOMA (Defense of Marriage Act), and witnessed the rise of a new Black Power movement led by black trans and queer women. In this second decade of the new millennium, we had to consider: how are Pilipinxs actively making sense of their his/herstories? And more importantly, how can we document it?

In this evolution of being Pilipina/o/x American, in this historical moment, we ask:" *What are Pilipinxs in these times envisioning for their communities? What is your vision? What are you thinking about? On this continuing journey across our communities, what now lies in your radical imaginations?*" In essence, "*What does it mean to be a Filipino... now?*"

It is overwhelming to think of how to introduce the following incredible pieces because the pieces speak for themselves. Unpacking many layers to the dimensions of our human existence and experiences that shape how we go about in this world is a difficult endeavor to repeat without taking the learnings out of context from the original source. I am so grateful for the community that came to speak our truths. May you feel the labor of love put forth from our contributors. They are testimonies of healing.

The Way We Flow

The book flows through five sections which reflect non-linearly how one might come to their own radicalization. Chapter 1– "Cutting Out a Space: Diaspora & Memory" begins to unpack identity by offering meditations on the ways in which we (have had to) travel through the world, as well as travel through memory to see more clearly where/who we are. Chapter 2– "To Breathe: Health & Well Being" explores our human condition as we slide between joy and grief, feeding our bodies with the goodness of food and community along the way. Chapter 3 – "Suturing our Split Selves: On Intersectionality" reveals stories of navigating other powerful social locations we occupy alongside our Pilipinx-ness, such as being a person of mixed heritage, or a person exploring sexual orientation and non-normative, queer love. Chapter 4– "Cause a Stir: Coalitional Consciousness & Organizing" suggests ways to think about collectivizing towards uplifting the spirits and changing the material conditions of our people. Lastly, Chapter 5– "How to Make Home: Family and Radical Parenting" models practices of resistance with those we love in a shared effort to build a new world, as they say, "the revolution begins at home."

The themes lay out the possibility of a narrative of radical healing in which a Pilipinx is jolted into (1) a memory of "home" or "the motherland," thus launching their (2) healing journey—one that requires they (3) put back together the pieces of themselves which have been ripped apart through legacies of colonialism. (4) The healing may happen through forms of collectivizing our voices and making calls to action; and at some point, may ultimately bring us to create new critically informed ways of (5) raising our families.

This book offers a weaving of stories from voices today we don't often hear. It's intended to add to the dialogue and build understandings that can bear out new relationships to the term Filipino American, Pin@y, Pilipina/o/x in this historical moment. We've never been a monolithic group or for that matter homogeneous. Our various ethnicities, regional backgrounds, relationships to religion, gender, politics, and class throw us into different corners. I think of Lola Eudocia[3] and the many other Pinays on the margins, never given air time for their stories to be told in their voices. Indeed, we have something to say. Our heterogeneous, hybrid, multiple groups within are responding to this world by spelling out our conflicting realities. All that is echoing inside us. Our concerns, hopes, dreams, aches, pains, efforts and triumphs as a people are published daily via social media. We are rising and falling, and we are watching each other.

We are taking note of the multitude of expressions of: our queer love and our transphobia; our support for Black Lives Matter, and our anti-blackness; our holistic healing practices, and our right to bear arms. All of this, as we tumble through the daily spectacle of the Trump administration and the Duterte administration after eight straight years of hope with Obama. The tide is changing. Fast. It pushes a quality of radical thought markedly different than any other time before. So from the corner coffeeshop to our living rooms to our classrooms, we are saying something. We are writing and creating with an urgency to push back on that which harms us, and with a promise to take care of ourselves. This is not a race. We will not run our spirits to the ground. We are working this shit out.

When Words Become Action

As you turn the pages of this reader, note that what is "radical" is up to you. It is a term with a hundred possibilities. Ultimately, the purpose of this reader is to stir conversation around the ever dynamic definition of who we are. It is you who identifies what needs more exploration and

---

[3] Tizon, A. (2017, June). My Family's Slave. The Atlantic . Retrieved July 31, 2017, from https://www.theatlantic.com/magazine/archive/2017/06/lolas-story/524490/

discussion: what is not said in this reader? What can be more deeply challenged or understood? What voices are not being included or honored? In here, our conversations emerge as we search for forms of wholeness, balance, justice, and love among us. We excavate truths about ourselves and our genealogies (of body, mind, and soul), birthing new language and ways of being that reflect this historical moment. We testify. Through memory and foresight. This book is a living, breathing time capsule capturing our fluidity in our process of becoming. May it honor and recognize our uniqueness as individuals in our commitment to connectedness. What is certain is that we are rising as critical beings: critical of history, critical of time, critical of space, and most importantly critical of ourselves. This book is made out of and made for our community: LOVE is the center and source. We wish you blessings as you read this book. If triggered, hold yourself tight. In the words of loving meditation: "May we live in this world with ease, happiness, and good health."

Peace & Light,
Melissa-Ann Nievera-Lozano

CUTTING OUT A SPACE:
DIASPORA
&
MEMORY

A Reunion of Strangers

Oscar Peñaranda

The U.S.-Philippines War and experience of the birth of Philippine Independence were still fresh in the minds of everyone when my father was born in 1904. In our hometown of Barugo, Leyte, my father's generation only remembers those days silently. My grandfather was a revolutionary leader who was reputedly the last of Aguinaldo's officers to lay down his arms. His son, my own father, never spoke about those days to me. I had to find out for myself how life was during the U.S.-Philippines war.

Silence was the source of many historical gaps, like the story of Philippine Independence, upon whose principles my lolo and many other Filipinos like him, fought so fiercely. As a writer and an educator, I have decided to break that silence.

Twenty years ago, Abe Ignacio, colleague, historian, author and librarian, called me from out of the blue and told me that he had just seen on eBay, a Filipino flag dated 1899 with the name "Peñaranda" written on it. He thought that was my lolo's flag, captured by the Americans during his battles against them, and that I should bid for it before someone else got it. I had never heard of this flag or any stories related to it from my lolo.

Last year in Dumaguete, Negros Oriental, this flag and I had a rendezvous with destiny.

The gathering, of course, was not planned at all. We—Nonoy del Prado, the hotel owner; Edo and Annabelle Adriano; Jose Manuel "Dong" Villegas; Alexander Bautista Bayot France; and I—arrived in front of the Florentina Hotel of Dumaguete within five minutes of each other. I had met Alex France 48 hours earlier, Dong not at all, Annabelle and Edo last year via text by a mutual friend Krip Yuson, and Nonoy, was the kind of person you thought you had met before but were not quite sure. Alex had never met any of them.

Alex, a Filipino martial arts master and teacher, had moved to nearby Sibulan three years earlier. A Caviteño by origin, he had lived in the US almost all his life and had come to retire there although he had no apparent link to the area. I came to see about an appointment in Silliman University. Like Alex, I am a student and advocate of Filipino martial arts. Nonoy had taken up some form of martial arts in his youth and was very interested in taking it up again, along with his son, Ramon, who had taken the "stick" fighting arts but stopped because of dengue fever and had been looking for a way to get back into it. Right away, father and son enrolled themselves in a private class with Alex.

In the midst of our conversation, I mentioned how about 20 years ago, I missed a bid on a certain invaluable family item on eBay, then a new on-line auction site, because of my incompetence with computers. And I paid a heavy price for that shortcoming. It never really left my mind. The item was a Filipino flag dated 1899 with the name *Peñaranda* handwritten on it, an obvious item identifier by whoever retrieved the flag. My heart had jumped upon seeing the item.

My grandfather, Florentino Peñaranda (Florentino is also my father's name and my middle name) had fought the U.S. fiercely for Philippine Independence at the turn of the 20th century and was reputedly the last officer of Aguinaldo's regular army to surrender, a year and a half after Aguinaldo himself, after Lukban, after Mojica, and after Malvar. But alas, not knowing how to bid on eBay, I could not procure his flag, a symbol of his legacy. I, however, wrote the seller and the eBay people to tell whoever had bought the flag that I am the grandson of Peñaranda, and that my family would be forever grateful if the buyer would contact me. I got no response.

As mentioned, I am also an educator in the U.S. When one of my fellow educators found out about my going to Dumaguete, he suggested that I contact his friend Alexander Bautista Bayot France. The name rang a bell. The previous year, in Dumaguete when I met Edo and Annabelle,

The full flag right side up with the red on top, symbolizing war. The author and his relatives are still trying to decipher what the symbol in the middle means.

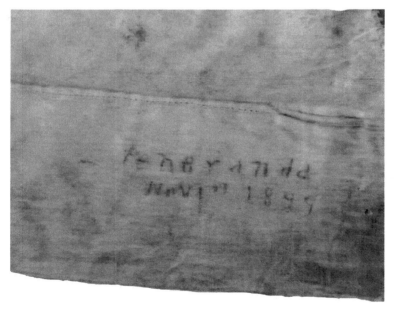

Close-up of handwritten name "Peñaranda" with date "Nov 1st 1899."
(PHOTOS BY I. VER)

I had walked along the Boulevard one Sunday morning and was eating at the Bethel Hotel when I saw a group of stick-fighters practicing by the tall treesalong the Boulevard. I approached them, and the instructor said that his name was Leonardo de la Luna. He told me that a colleague of his was also from the States, like me, but was now living in the Dumaguete area, one Alexander Bautista Bayot France. He gave me his card.

Alex picked me up from the Dumaguete airport. When we were having a late lunch, he said he knew Leonardo quite well and that he also wanted to talk about another topic. It was then that he broached a question that caught me off-guard. "What do you know about the Peñaranda family?" he asked. I said I knew about our private family history and my lolo's role in the fight for independence, though it was hardly in any history books.

I thought Alex was interested in a business proposal of some sort. He said, "I know about your lolo." How? "I believe I have your grandfather's flag. I was the one who outbid everybody to get his flag on eBay." I was floored. A mountain was lifted off my long-burdened heart.

"I put all my month's salary (without telling my wife, of course) to make sure that I outbid all those war memorabilia collectors," Alex said. "When I was bidding for that flag, I was thinking that since the Americans had taken that flag from the Filipinos, I was going to liberate it from its American captors." He also said that an acquaintance who had owed him a longstanding debt of a thousand dollars had, from out of the blue, paid him within a week of this purchase.

I told Alex that one of my missions in the Philippines was to put up a plaque in the typhoon-ravaged Baybay Municipal Building where my lolo brought his people to surrender on June 19, the day after his 25th birthday, and where he made his final and gallant speech as the last holdout of that gruesome war. My friend Joe Robles, another Fil-Am now retired in Baybay, was going to help me, I told Alex. "I know Joe quite well," he said. "Good man." Another surprise. I didn't realize he knew Joe. "When you and your family get that plaque built, it would be my honor to give that flag to your family. For then, at long last, it would have found its true home."

By the time we meandered our separate ways home past midnight, Alex and I felt like old friends. We probably were. That is, our souls were like flitting butterflies hovering around our destinies before we physically met.

But it took Dumaguete to introduce all of us to each other and to discover our past lives.

When I got back to the States, Alex and I did not communicate for about a month. He had told me that when I returned to San Francisco, he will tell his grandson in Vallejo my contact numbers and he can arrange with me how to let me have the flag. I met the grandson Isiah on Sutter St. in a college he was attending. He came out and with a bow, handed me the flag encased in a triangular container with a plastic glass window. The flag was visible but it was all folded. I did not open the case until it was time to take a picture of it for this article.

The day I got it, I carried the encased banner with me without missing the grand irony of it all: that this same Philippine flag captured by U.S. soldiers who had embarked from this city of San Francisco to the battlefields of the Philippines to fight the Filipinos whose leader's grandson now walk these same streets with the same flag retrieved and recovered from U.S. possession and history.

MaryCarl Guiao

Atang for Apu

past is awake, alive
She secures ties—loving, ancestral, cultural, purest—amongst Us.
heart mentor, visionary
sobrang da ka miss na miss
She teaches value of the genuine, constructive interpersxnal
like Francisco Dagohoy's well-grounded, undying spirit.
honored to be of Her
of a principled industrious empowering sensitivity
of transformative depth
of the mate-canon-manduhit-courage kind;
honored to be of the same surviving clan, tribe, intricate spiritual
elements.
miss da ka kawlan at umpang uman
ing sucal ning lub cu
resisting everyday societal barriers pushing Our alienation fr Her
authentic love
all part and parcel of properly mourning for Her
palagi da kang kalaguran

past, current, projected
repression degradation dehumxnization
blindly following religion / just follower types
prevented too many of Us fr being w You & taking care of You as You
deserve.
wider relations/systems of power must allow Us All true freedom to
choose
to live-out being w ating mga Lolas;
must support reindigenization, self determination, undoing eurocentric
lotsa-times-covert-&-"benevolent" all-ways-violent assimilation;
must forever work to ensure being worthy of being at chosen-ally status

imprints of toxic imposed-over-Us white masculine authority in my blood.
the story since european conquest-&-commerse-fueled(-&-sustained—
ie, continuously exponentially worsening) contact.
eg, america's "White Man's Burden" justifying war on Our Motherland, 15
yrs of
Our homes being burnt to the ground and Our loved ones being shot;
racializing/otherizing Us as barbaric or improper or unclean or
ignorant anti-expansionist or isang "mas mababang anyo" ng hayop
(eg, noisome reptile, stubborn donkey, unruly dog).
so much of Our
colonized-imperialized-by-western-capitalist-ventures-roman-
catholic-&-angelican-led-institutes herstory/TheirStory/OurStory
included
portraying Pinays, esp native womxn of Maharlikha, as not humxn,
entirely born to be prostitutes, born nannies, geisha like, inferior,
uncivilized.
You countered these poisonous cruel consciousnesses

medicinal wisdom-keeper Spirit
amidst a world of suffocating prejudice;
amidst being relegated to a neutralized insignificance at society's out
edges,
crushing reincarnations of The Katipunan;
amidst Our loved ones from the South being displaced and uprooted
by global destructions such as international treaties
that place corporate rights & freedoms above all life, all people;
amidst wounds we (in all too many cases, are groomed to) inflict on
Ourselves
and wounds (identical to the aforementioned wounds by their
cause-&-effect)
inflicted on generations to come.
the pain of the womxn of Betis, of Maharlikha, of Her growing up. as an
adult.
lacking Dagami-like revoltz (though-w-follow-throughs)
fraught w desperately-in-need-of-an-alt-to globalization and vapid
departure

from the Dukit tradition,
from Indigenous & Our more modern critical consciousness paradigms

with You, grand antitdote
my process, smooth
to get at the deep rooted "logic"of unrestrained excessive
domination/ownership
that threatens Mama Earth, all non animal & animal beings.
a source of healing stories, of rhythms of recovery
engaging me away
from a mainstreamed culture of trauma X emotional immaturity
that perpetrate colonizations, including deprecating internalizations.
daya mi cacawal.
empress roots Mama
if it were dismantled, sana
we wouldnt have to be preoccupied, inside & out.
I'd keep You as safe as possible, napakaligtas and in your element.
parati
mahal na mahal na mahal kita
kalaguran da ka sobra sobra Apu Liling

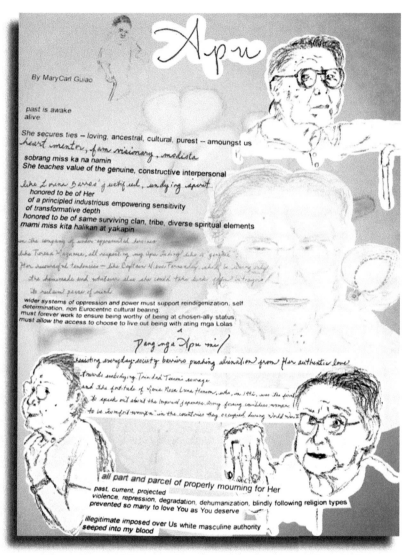

My earlier, graphic expression of my "Apu" poem to it's evolution
(see transcription) to how I perform it today.

The Kapampangan word "Apu" translated into English is
grandparent/grandmother/grandfather/elder.

Home

Rovielle Yamaki

Childhood was an array of colourful memories like jeepneys, green mangoes on sticks, extended families, bbq-smelling street food, warm tropical nights and organized chaos. That was the Philippines for me. The familiarity of it was home.

Around the age of nine in 1991 my family and I immigrated to Australia, the continent known as 'Down Under'. The twist of coming from a mono-cultured country to a multicultural city set the course of my search to *find my truth*. I was very confused initially.

The Escalante family settled in the clean, quiet suburbs of orderly Melbourne. This city is renowned to have four seasons in a day. How true! The pale-skinned faces of people with strange-coloured eyes made me feel awkward and in wonder. School years exposed to me that though I could fit in within a very Anglo-Saxon world, I still stood out.

Thank goodness for my Filipina genes that can adapt, with humour and food, when faced with any challenge. The Australian accent came naturally and long before I knew it, I would mutter, "No worries, mate!", "She'll be right!" and "G'day". Tagalog was shared at home with my parents but I reverted to English with my siblings Paolo and Danielle. Somehow, this suited us. Being bilingual empowered me. By the time I graduated from Melbourne University my mind thought Aussie.

I pursued a career in Japan, which brought yet again another culture shock. Written Japanese looked nothing like alphabet letters. Locals greeted each other with a bow and shoes were taken off inside every home, in schools and even at offices. Traditional tea shops steamed with delectable aromas, desserts were served like elegant art and gardens immaculately manicured. It was a country of organisation in the highest order.

The joke was I looked Asian enough to blend in, but was still considered a complete stranger. To add confusion to my self-esteem, when I visited the Philippines and spoke Tagalog, my Aussie twang set me apart from the rest of my family.

What a conundrum!

So I took a good look at myself and asked the question instead…"If home is nowhere and everywhere, how do I make the most of it?"

Together, with my Japanese husband, Kentaro and I concocted a radical lifestyle change from city to countryside. In the warmer climate of the Sunshine Coast, in a tiny nestled paradise called Crystal Waters Ecovillage, we learned how to quieten our minds, grow our self-confidence and re-discover *self-worthiness.*

Through networking systems like 'Willing Workers On Organic Farms', Permaculture communities and house-sitting which, depended on trusting 'strangers' and taking a leap of faith, a whole new world emerged. We ate fresh vegetables and fruits from lush gardens, awakened to the songs of birds, gazed at grazing kangaroos and slept to the sound of frogs, crickets and under the serenity of the tender moon. And if during the day the sun got sweltering hot, we dipped in a creek flowing with cool pristine water. Eventually, we gained the trust of the community and forged friendships. Then, we built a small farm where we grew and supplied from, edamame beans and our own miso paste. Nature Kids was a program we facilitated before finally extending ourselves by serving locals and tourists wholesome food from our first family-run business called, 'Soul about Sushi' in the heart of our township. And, a very special little person Cocomi Elle, our one-year old daughter, decided to join us for the ride!

Philippines, Japan, Australia… What a world richly infused with traditions, values, and expressions. I am forever grateful to Rolando and Maria Violeta, my parents who were brave enough to step into *the beyond* to a land of many chances for success. The interesting part is that, from my life's adventure of intertwined confusion and cultivation, I have come to realize that Home is what you *create* it to be.

*From left—daughter Cocomi Elle (6 months), Rovielle & husband Kentaro
at their SOUL ABOUT SUSHI kiosk in the heart of Maleny town, in Australia.*

paintings from memory

Nicole Gervacio

The following paintings are based off family photographs from
the Philippines. The figures of these portraits are not fully realized and are
almost invisible. The edges of their form disappear but our imagination makes
up for what is implied. These images represent the difficulty in uncovering
one's heritage as a first-generation Pilipinx American

young girl and almost woman

embrace

the monteclaros

four men

*This image also represents an unawareness of the roles Pilipinx's
have had in American and world history.*

The Filipino/Pilipina/Pin@y/Pinxy (American) Aswang: Imagining Identity in Diaspora

Joseph Allen Ruanto-Ramirez

*MA, PhD student in Cultural Studies – American Studies,
Claremont Graduate University*

To Love as Aswang (2015) became a momentous moment for many Pilipinx American youths as it combines the poetic language of Barbara Jane Reyes and the imaginary of what an Aswang (also spelled as Asuwang) is or are. Though many researchers have contested what exactly is an Aswang, regional and ethnic definitions throughout the Bisayas and Luzon has always played it in the minds and hearts of many Pilpinx and even Pilpinx Americans. The image of an Aswang ranges from a demon-like woman severed from the waste with bat wings to a shape-shifting ghoul that tricks its prey. Aswang (pl) is never just one thing, one identity, or one definition. It is not all this yet all of this, something more yet something unknown. It straddles between the imaginary and the reality, the historical and the contemporary, the natural and the spiritual. The Aswang is complex. It is much, much more than what can be written in this paper or in any text, yet also unexplainable through oral traditions and artistic expressions. Here, I briefly argue that the Aswang is more than what we think, yet nothing at the same time.

The term Aswang came from the Sanskrit word for Asura which means "demon." Various accounts and regional descriptions of the Aswang through Central and Northern Philippines makes "it" undefinable yet each ethnic group and region has a definite description of it. Aswang (pl) has been tied to ancient women priestesses and shamans who were cut from the waist up by the Spanish and therefore their spirits haunts the living (Manananggal). Another look at Aswang is through the demon child Tiyanak who sucks the fetus from the woman's body resulting in miscarriages or the Tikbalang, a demon with the upper body of a horse and legs of a man. Aswang seems to take a form of something that is hybrid— the living dead, an animal/human fusion, and a non-human who needs the essence/soul/blood of the living. They do so not necessarily to kill, but to survive, to exist, to continue living, to make sure their relevance (regardless of how demonic or fearful they may be) is still important. So what then is an Aswang and how does it relate to Philippine–America? Can I argue that Pilipinx Americans are exactly that, also less, yet a bit more? Are Pilipinx Americans Aswang (pl)?

I play with the Post-Humanist (sometimes read as "Un-Human" Studies") theories and look at how these monsters, demons, figments of our imaginations are actually more than that; it is actually a manifestation of us. The Aswang, in the form of the Manananangal, was severed from the waist; her lower body wanders the land as her upper body flies through the air searching for her prey. She was the healer, the cultural bearer, the leader, the educated, the astronomer, the artist that the Spaniards and Catholicism wished to silence, oppress, and erase. She was colonized and split in half, one bound to the earth, the other travelled and transverse. She is killed by what is considered pure, holy, and, by extension, civilized. The Pilipinx American is also severed—cut from the spirit and the mind, where they long to know the past, the precolonial, the indigenous while living in the land of the colonizer. They are colonized; their tongues severed just enough to not speak with other Aswang (pl), but can still mutter enough to sound like one. They straddle multiple realms and lands, across waters and skies, trying to look for their bottom half that is still attached to the land their ancestors came from, one day hoping to stand completely as their ancestors did (Shohat, 2006).

Like the Tiyanak, the Pilipinx American Aswang is infantilized— seen as a child that needs to be educated, civilized, Americanized. It longs to connect to the bodies that know what life is, what being Pilipinx means. They absorb the works of authors and scholars that has written about them, their communities, their histories, their identities.

They mimic the dances from the Philippines and perform them as a way to connect to their semi-lost identities. They devour anything and everything that may would give them a sense of belonging and a sense of self. They are childlike not because they are immature or uneducated, but because, sometimes, being marked as an adult means that these longings are expected to be hobbies rather than finding one self. "Adult" means they are marked to be "mature" and therefore these imaginings of the yester-life and longing for pre-colonial should be let go to make way for fiscal and familial success. To marry and be an adult means to grow up, and therefore, imagining becomes a hobby that can only be invoked on free time.

Like the Tikbalang, it is a hybrid of the natural and unnatural, of human and animal, of imaginary and reality, a hybrid, a chimera (Haraway, 1991). They live in mountains and tall trees, hiding from others knowing that if they reveal themselves, they will be feared and destroyed. Yet can you really kill a Tikbalang? It is said that when it rains while the sun is out, a Tikbalang is born. A Tikbalang is born from the mixing and existence of two unnatural (yet very natural) events. The Pilipinx American exists as a child of the indigenous and the colonizer, of the East and the West, of life and the bringer of "death." Both the Tiyanak and the Tikbalang are "dead," not because they are physically dead, but because they are seen as non-human. Only humans are marked for "life," to exist, to continue, they are marked for "death" because their whole existence draws fear from the living and their bodies are needed to be disposed as a means to purify the living's reality (Mbembe, 2003).

I argued that the Aswang (pl) are dead, but not just because they are demons or ghouls, but because they are bound to death and will continue living knowing they are marked as dead (Byrd, 2011). The Pilipinx American Aswang IS dead. They are constantly "killed," bound to a system that marks them as unnarrated bodies, numbers and data for statistics, and consumed into a system that washes away their "brownness" and placing them into a Model Minority caste that will one day let go of their cultural baggage and become American. They continue living and find themselves in a system that has marked them as bodies (and a community) that are disposable. Like the Manananangal, their entrails still exist. These entrails are the physical manifestations of what the subject needs to survive, to live, and without them, the subject "dies" or is minimized. These entrails are not just the Manananggal's liver and intestines, but are also the Pilipinx Aswang's cultural attire, broken language of their mother tongue, their food, the garlic smell of their house on a weekend morning's breakfast. They are in museums as "native artifacts," in history books that consist a couple of lines, and a corridor between the Pacific and the rest of Asia in a ride at Disneyland. Small manifestations of their existence, bound to a particular imagination that wishes to become a reality. They are marked for "death" because they very existence must be erased or minimized, never completely whole, never complete themselves. Holy water and crosses subdues them from quenching their thirst and filling their hunger to find themselves, to come out of hiding, to be themselves with everyone else being themselves. Like ghosts, these ghouls haunt every place they go to. Always saying their name, demanding to be seen, demanding their stories to be told, demanding to exist. Like ghosts, the Pilipinx American Aswang only wants justice in their names, their stories to be written down so others may know who they are, and their memories passed down. The Pilipinx American Aswang haunts every place they go to showing their existence with bumper stickers on their cars, tshirts, baseball hats, and tattoos. Their existence is never fully themselves as they always search for their true identity and its meaning (Gordon, 2008). The Pilipinx American Aswang is made up, yet real at the same time. It is a creation of the personal and communal, the cultural and the political, the imagined and the lived realities. They are both spatial and temporal—connected to land and through time. Manifested through tangible objects and a hybrid of indigenous and non-indigenous. It is exactly more than what can be explained on this paper. The Pilipinx American Aswang is who ever is reading this article and is also the writer—trying to find meaning and communicating with other Aswang (pl) through a language, a tongue that has been severed and speaks in other tongues, a language that is not theres. The Pinxy Aswang leaves their mark in this book, hoping one day to have a discussion with other Aswang (pl) even though their existence means they must feed off each other. The Aswang is dead and lives in a violent world haunting, feeding, existing…all this and more, but still incomplete.

Note: I use (pl) to denote plurality rather than adding an "s" as a norm in English lexicons.

REFERENCES

Byrd, Jodi A. 2011. *The Transit of Empire: Indigenous Critiques of Colonialism*. Minneapolis, MN: University of Minnesota Press.

Gordon, Avery. 2008. *Ghostly Matters: Haunting and the Sociological Imagination*. 2nd ed. Minneapolis, MN: University of Minnesota Press.

Haraway, Donna. 1991. "A Cyborg Manifesto: Science, Technology, and Socialist-Feminism in the Late Twentieth Century" in *Simians, Cyborgs and Women: The Reinvention of Nature*. New York, NY: Routledge. 149-181.

Mbembe, Achille. 2003. "Necropolitics." translated by Libby Meintjes. *Public Culture 15* (1): 11-40.

Reyes, Barbara Jane. 2015. *To Love as Aswang*. San Francisco, CA: PAWA, Inc.

Shohat, Ella. 2006. *Taboo Memories, Diasporic Voices*. Durham, NC: Duke University Press.

A Transnational Appreciation of Filipino and American Culture Through Music

BERNARD ELLORIN, PhD

This story chronicles my journey of appreciating my cultural heritage through music in the Filipino-American Diaspora. Throughout this lifelong learning experience, I have encountered many obstacles in the pursuit of having a career in ethnomusicology—the study of music as culture—as a traditional Philippine musician. Traversing the globe as a researcher and as a transnational Filipino is my contribution to the stories and articles in this book. Embracing Philippine culture through the arts while educating others in my community and in academia has ultimately been my chosen path to be successful in a country that renders Filipinos and Filipino-Americans invisible.

Raised in Southeast San Diego; Schooled in Different Neighborhoods

Born in Manila in the early 1980s, I immigrated to the United States when I was a year old. Under the Third Preference Immigration Act, my mother immigrated to this country as a working professional for the County of San Diego; to this day, she's actively involved in Filipino American community activities. Raised in Southeast San Diego with my three older siblings, I developed an appreciation for the diversity of my neighborhood of South Bay Terrace—an area predominantly populated by Blacks, Mexicans, and Filipinos. However, our experience being part of a marginalized ethnic minority in the United States was further heightened while attending secondary schools in white upper middle-class neighborhoods.

I attended schools in the predominantly white neighborhoods of Point Loma and University City under the Voluntary Enrollment Exchange Program (VEEP). This experience taught me how to assert my ethnic identity at an early age among individuals ignorant about culture. Between the 1980s and 1990s, when I attended grade school, there were hardly any representations of Filipinos or Filipino American culture in the media. Whenever I told someone "I'm Filipino," my classmates, and to some extent, my teachers, uttered the following stereotypes: "Wow I love pancit and lumpia," "Aren't most of you dog-eaters?" and "you are from that country run by that woman who owns a thousand shoes"—all images most Filipinos were notorious for during that time period. Fortunately, my mother was heavily involved in community organizations that fostered awareness of Philippine cultural arts; the Samahan Filipino American Performing Arts and Education Center was an outlet for my Filipino American peers to learn about an idealized view of our culture and the arts.

The Samahan Filipino American Performing Arts & Education Center

"Instead of me learning how to play music—as a board member of Samahan—I enrolled my son in *rondalla* (Philippine stringed ensemble music) lessons with the education center so he can experience some aspect of Filipino culture through music; he is also taking piano lessons anyway," my mother recounts this story whenever she explains to others why she has a son passionate about Philippine music here in the United States. Like many Asian American youth, I learned how to play the piano—my first musical instrument. After a few months of learning compositions from Western classical and romantic period composers—Mozart, Beethoven, and Tchaikovsky—my mother thought it would be a good idea to enroll me in rondalla music lessons in order to appreciate some aspects of Filipino culture. At the age of 10, I learned how to play the *banduria*—a fourteen-stringed Filipino-style mandolin and the main melodic instrument to a rondalla ensemble—with Dr. Juanita Caccam, aka "Auntie

Nita," the rondalla instructor of the Samahan. I remember my initial encounter with the banduria: my fingers hurt from pressing on the frets of those metal strings. Auntie Nita assured me, "Once you start practicing regularly, you will get used to it." This experience symbolized the learning process of appreciating and advocating for Filipin@ culture in the United States; continue to persevere to succeed regardless of any setbacks or obstacles that come your way.

Rondalla lessons with the education center laid the foundation for having knowledge of some aspect of life in the Philippine countryside, the Spanish and American colonization. As a *rondalla* student, I learned how Filipinos took aspects of their colonial heritage and made it distinctly their own to fit the climate of a tropical maritime Southeast Asian nation. Exposure to an indigenous form of Philippine music began when I became a student of kulintang (gong-chime music) with Maguindanaoan master musician, Danongan Kalanduyan. Through strict and rigorous training from Kalanduyan, I realized how indigenous Philippine ethnic groups, such as the Maguindanao, resisted colonization and were proud of maintaining their traditional heritage with its own level of sophistication. This dichotomy led to the acknowledgement of the Philippines as a heterogeneous nation that is often misunderstood as homogenous. With this need to be respectful to all aspects of Philippine culture, I made a concerted effort to conduct my own research while acknowledging the native practitioners I studied under both in the Philippines and in the Diaspora. In my community, I established the Pakaraguian Kulintang Ensemble as an outlet for learning about traditional and cultural aspects of southern Philippine gong-row music with respect for the master artists and native practitioners I have been privileged to learn from in the United States and the Philippines. Conducting annual research with a critical mindset was what trained me to pursue college degrees in ethnomusicology.

Ethnomusicology

As the principal rondalla and kulintang musician of Samahan, the education center was invited to perform for international events throughout

Southern California. As a performer I gained exposure to various traditional musicians from many parts of the world. The All Nations International Dance and Music Festival enabled me to experience cultural performances from various groups—Teye Sa Thiosanne African Drum & Dance Company West African percussionists, mariachi and Ballet Folklorico Mexican-American ensembles, South Indian classical dancing and music from the Patnaik Sisters, and Brazilian samba hegue ensembles—were some of performing arts organizations I had the pleasure of sharing the stage with as I "represented the Philippines" with Samahan. Observing the diversity of music through these intersections developed my initial interest in ethnomusicology.

As a student at Southwestern Community College, I researched on which four-year universities offered ethnomusicology; University of California Los Angeles (UCLA) was the pioneering university to establish the discipline. Transferring to UCLA to major in ethnomusicology developed my theoretical framework of conceptualizing music form other cultures; at the same time, I learned how to represent and educate others on the importance of Philippine culture as the token Filipino ethnomusicologist.

Graduate studies and community work

After receiving my Bachelors in ethnomusicology from UCLA, I took the advice to pursue my graduate degrees at a university that focuses on music in the Asia-Pacific region. The University of Hawaii at Manoa proved to be the ideal choice since I would be under the supervision of Ricardo D. Trimillos—the leading Philippine American Ethnomusicologist in the United States. Under Trimillos I had my experience teaching and theorizing about Philippine music. Through his tutelage I also learned how to balance between being an academic and community performer. While I had a wealth of experience as a performer, I needed to complement that experience with making it understandable to communities at-large.

Choosing Philippine music as my area of specialty in graduate school enabled me to develop my transnational framework of research. I benefited from receiving research grants abroad in order to maintain cross-cultural relations with my fellow *kababayan* in the homeland who are master artists in their communities As a researcher, I learned that I am part of a larger movement for Philippine ethnomusicologists and native practitioners to provide scholarly material in order for our culture to be recognized globally and in the larger academic sphere. Networking with Philippine scholars at the University of the Philippines and connecting with master artists directly in the field—both in northern Luzon and the southern Philippines—were the initial steps I took to maintain connections with like-minded scholars espousing cultural preservation in their own communities. More importantly, the need for academics of color is a necessity that remains to be seen; hence, this was the impetus for obtaining both my masters and PhD in the Arts and Humanities.

Concluding thoughts

In order for the Filipino American community to be visible we need to maintain a sense of balance between appreciating our culture and being aware of our privileges here in the United States that we should use to our advantage in succeeding as a Diasporic community. Living in the United States poses challenges for many of us to be respected as a marginalized community; succeeding in our lives through education and pursuing our passion in any field will render us visible. My experience as a Diasporic Filipino American musician Philippine musician functioning in the academic and in the cultural realm has positioned me in various settings that have taken me to different parts of the world.

Remaining true to my roots and positionality—a 1.5 Filipino American young adult—has driven me to pursue a higher degree as an academic of color. I envision many Filipino American youth maintaining that appreciation for their culture and their American heritage as we become visible in the media and in any chosen profession. In conclusion, as long we remain grounded and rooted we can be successful as a community who can uplift others who feel the need to assimilate while not having a drive or passion to succeed.

Commencement Speech
for College of Computer Studies IT
Pamantasan ng Lungsod ng Pasig
City of Pasig University
Pasig, Metro Manila
Thursday, April 7, 2016, at 1PM

JULIUS PARAS
*Senior Vice President for Customer Engagement
& Country Manager, Philippines
Kalibrr*

Thank you for the kind introduction.

Good afternoon, President Alcantara, Vice President Pagulayan, Dean Arcangel, PLP staff, Mayor Eusebio. Moreso, good afternoon to our graduates and their families. It's truly an honor to be invited to speak to you today, especially as I am neither an information technology graduate, nor a graduate of this University.

Several years ago, I graduated from Stanford University, with a degree in Industrial Engineering. I took two courses in software engineering. That's it.

HOWEVER, I did spend an entire career in IT with a legendary company who saw me as a "diamond in the rough." After failing to impress recruiters at several companies, I was eventually hired by Hewlett-Packard, the original Silicon Valley technology "garage" startup, as an IT Business Analyst months before my own commencement ceremony. During my last term at school, I would wake up early and go to work, while other students were either sleeping or attending class. From that single opportunity, I was able to build an IT career that spanned almost 15 years, to travel throughout the US and parts of India, and to learn lessons that I still find very useful.

Today, I want to share THREE of those lessons with you.

"Get Over Yourself"

I knew about HP ever since I was in high school. I was fascinated by their calculators which had no equals sign. They used a method called "Reverse Polish Notation" (RPN for short), and in order to add 2 and 2 together, instead of typing "2+2=" you would type in "2enter2+". So what, what's the difference? There are 4 keystrokes for this expression, but when you want to do longer calculations, it actually saves time using this method by using less keystrokes.

On my first day, at a company that I DIDN'T think would hire me, I came VERY prepared. I shined my black shoes to where you could see your reflection in them. I wore a tie. I brought the briefcase that my father had given me as a gift for college. I think I even arrived an hour early. In short, I spent the first day and many months trying to follow instructions and do exactly what was expected of me by my manager. I was proud to have this new kind of work.

BEFORE THIS JOB, to earn extra money, I washed dishes, waited tables, and worked cash registers. I was able to get this job along with people who had majored in Information Systems or had already earned their MBAs. I made good money—enough to pay back my student loans and to save money for myself and my family. I was happy.

A few months into my routine, I had a senior level manager approach with some unexpected feedback. She was in another part of our corporate headquarters, and I didn't work closely with her. But, one day, she pulled me aside and said to me, "Julius, you need to make more of an impact." I was surprised, and I felt bad. I thought I was doing everything right, and she was saying I wasn't doing enough.

After sorting through my feelings of self-doubt and frustration, I came to the understanding that she was really trying to help me. What she meant is that I needed to get to know colleagues outside my own group, to understand my customers as well as their customers, and to clearly report the results to which I was directly contributing. It was good professional and business advice. I JUST HAD TO OVERCOME MY OWN EGO TO ACCESS IT. That's my first lesson… "just get over yourself."

"Work Yourself Out of a Job"

My next lesson happened a few years later, after changing managers a few times, and going through numerous organizational changes. In Silicon Valley, people know that startups quickly change, but large multinational corporations go through their fair share of changes, too.

At that time, I was lucky to have a manager who was also a mentor and coach. As minorities in a white, male-dominated tech culture, we were able to share stories and struggles of having different personal backgrounds than most others in our company. Through our shared stories, she and I identified as much with the people cleaning our offices at night as much as those who occupied them in the day.

This manager challenged me to add a new goal to every project I led, and THAT goal was to eliminate my own job. That's right. To constantly put myself out of work became my goal.

This challenge was actually a few lessons wrapped into one. If one fundamental business operations objective is to do more, with less, it just makes sense to enable others to be successful when you are no longer around. As either IT professionals or aspiring IT professionals, we know that the systems we design should be able to work with minimal maintenance, support, and manual intervention.

Another important lesson was what does one do when left without a job? The answer is to embrace new challenges.

"Be Comfortable with Being Uncomfortable"

This last lesson is one of the most difficult to learn. Embracing new challenges involves learning to be comfortable with being uncomfortable.

Discomfort creates stress. No one likes stress. Whether physical or mental, stress and prolonged stress (or struggle) are painful. They take a toll on us, and it hurts.

In the business world, much of the challenges arise from leadership decisions and working with colleagues to plan for and execute on them.

For example, what markets to pursue? Where to locate your business operations? What kind of people to hire? Otherwise, we are challenged by the everyday tasks of working in teams, across teams, or with people outside of our own organization. None of these are easy.

For better or worse, I approach discomfort as a feedback mechanism for something I either have to take action on or accept about myself. It takes practice to know the difference and perhaps a certain amount of emotional intelligence, but it's always worth the individual effort.

So, learning to be comfortable with being uncomfortable until taking action. That's the third lesson.

Why These Lessons?

I shared these 3 lessons because now is a very special time—not just for you and your families, but also for the Philippines and its neighbors in the ASEAN region, namely Brunei, Indonesia, Malaysia, Singapore, Cambodia, Laos, Myanmar, and Vietnam. With a total population second only to China and India, this region is the 7th largest economy in the world.

As college graduates, you become part of a special group of people. Of everyone in the world, only 7% are graduates of universities of colleges. And, even a smaller percentage, of course, are graduates of Information Technology.

Your next challenges will relate to these three lessons of (1) how to make an impact while overcoming your ego, (2) what kind of work to pursue -- whether you have work or not, and (3) how to handle all the challenges that you will face.

As Filipinos, engaging other cultures and overcoming challenges has historically been part of our collective struggles... AND successes. We experienced tremendous changes during the Spanish colonial period, World War II, and even now with the economic focus shifting to Asia.

And, finally, graduates, I am here to remind you of one key thing. You're not alone. Let me repeat, you are not alone in facing these challenges.

Now, just for a minute. Take a look at the person to your left. Then, to your right. Just look around at this crowd of over 600 family, friends, classmates, teachers, and supporters. Even my work at Kalibrr is to help people exactly like you—young, smart, and motivated—to identify these new opportunities for the rest of your careers.

SO, let us commence... together. Right here. Right now.

Thank you all. Maraming salamat, and congratulations, again, to you the Class of 2016.

Janna Añonuevo Langholz

Untitled (from series Cutting Out a Space), 2011
Gelatin silver print, 11x14 in

I create temporary installations and performances in spaces that have
been forgotten or abandoned. Spaces like these in transition offer a
place for the construction of imagined worlds, where the possibilities
for change and growth are infinite. Like the paper, these spaces can
be taken over by anything that chooses to occupy them, becoming a
framework for a place to call our own.

PELE PAGASA

Almost a year ago, I moved back to the original land of my parents and ancestors, the Philippines. These lyrics are excerpts taken from verses and songs I wrote over the years, old and new. Life reflections, conversations and stories processed through rap form. What do I envision? Freedom, justice and dignity for the majority oppressed and exploited in our nation and around the world. The future of our children and the planet are depending on us.

Sacrifice today, so tomorrow's not a dream

"Before Islam and the Muslims,
Christians and the missions,
We were worshiping the sun, farming and fishing,
listen to the elders passing on traditions,
family and barangay raising all the children,
praying to our ancestors knowing they are listening,"
providing us the answers, showing us why we living,
for the land, for the sea, for the sky….Family,
dignified reasons why we live and die naturally…"

"I was born and raised in the U-S-A,
Southeast San Diego, Californ-i-a,
first generation born far away,
7,000 miles so far away,
from the place where the rest of my family stays,
still this place has its place,
in my chest today…"

"How can I explain it,
amongst all this hatred,
the love you gave me sacred,
so the struggle I embraced it,
unplugged me from the matrix,
taught me principles thats basic,
be humble, disciplined, self critical and face it,
the path to liberation takes passion dedication,
constant contradictions, challenges is painstaking..."

Our people gonna win I promise we gonna take it back,
For our ancestors, our people, children and our land,
My kasamas use a gat if you must,
And I swear our people ain't asking for much,
All we want is our freedom,
freedom and the land,
Land that you stole..."

"A world full of boys and girls born into poverty,
no food in their stomachs millions deprived from democracy,
they survived this hypocrisy for generations on plantations,
parents till the land but in their hands receive no compensation,
no education, no healthcare, no food, no welfare,
the system shows it don't care, the children know this ain't fair.."

She was young fearless and thought nothing was impossible,
they called her dumb, careless, naive, not logical,
for choosing this path, but for her it wasn't optional,
to serve as a medic, but not in the hospital,

in villages seldom seen, so many obstacles,
climbing mountains crossing rivers and ravines,
never walking alone see she was part of a team,
I can only imagine all the beauty and struggle she seen,
but she embraced the sacrifice,
and never thought twice,
to give her life to the poor,
places where they never even seen a doctor before,
children dying of diseases that are easily cured,
this inhumane poverty is the rich man's war,
the have nots have nothing,
Still the rich want more?
She give her everything everyday defending the poor,
including her life,
another story of a revolutionary's sacrifice,
in this people's war…

I hope you learn to make it on your own,
And if you love your people,
Know you'll never be alone,
I hope that you get everything you want and that you chose,
I hope that it's the realest thing that you've ever known,
Hope we get to see our home and our people really free,
Sacrifice today then tomorrow's not a dream,
And when we win the rev just remember one thing,
Remember one thing,
We all can change the world,
We all must change this world.

W. Kyle De Ocera

Back to Self

I lost myself
On the path
To search for you

These steps
I walked for you
Led me
To catch
Judgment thrown

The unknown
Cut me

Heart
Is just
Muscle

Alone

Until
You
Know
What
It beats
For

No time to look
back
Stop or think

Push back
Towards brink
Of vanishing values
Sacred native tongue

trade

Fit and adapt
Yet Inept
Does it matter
The glass
Is half empty
Or half full
When it's
Not yours?

Pray

Here

Without home
Purpose doesn't exist
I am broken away
Into pieces of typecast
And clichés
An outcast
Transplant sacrifice
Of third world dreams
Accustomed to
Wearing masks
Flashy
Eloquent
And numb
On path of prescribed identity
Just don't look back
Don't
Look back

Pieces of
Migrant brown
Resist to forget
Protect innocence
Amidst flashy
Fast pace regret
Pieces of self
Further split apart
Third worlds
Away from heart

In the beginning
The child of sun
Smiled and Loved
With no qualms

Severed from
Roots
Where life
Hold ground
The cause
Origin
Of golden
Red-brown
Glow
When
Skin kiss
The sun
A magical spell
Educed
By melody
Of birthright
Song
Of belonging
Meant
To be sung

Until
Arrival

Kelan ka babalik?
(When are you returning?)
Was always asked

Because

Belonging

Wasn't

Going to be

Where
It was
Before
Damage:
To find

Self
Incomplete
From
Yesterday's lost
(Way back)
Been broken
(Way back)
Now look
(Way back)
To find
Way back

TO BREATHE:
HEALTH
&
WELL BEING

A Geography of My Own

by Trinidad Escobar

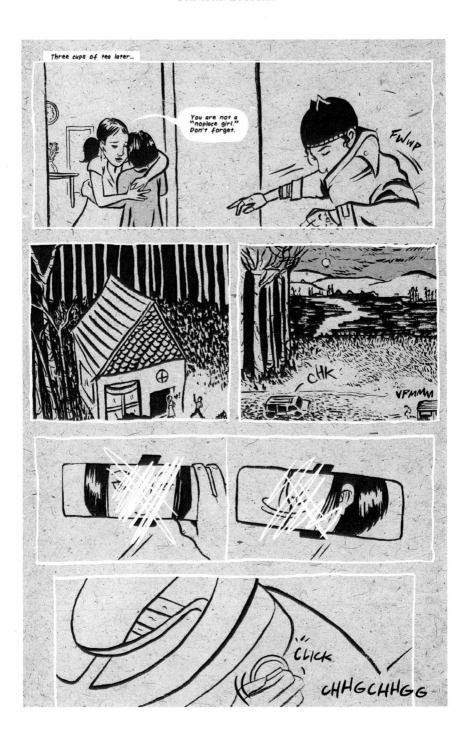

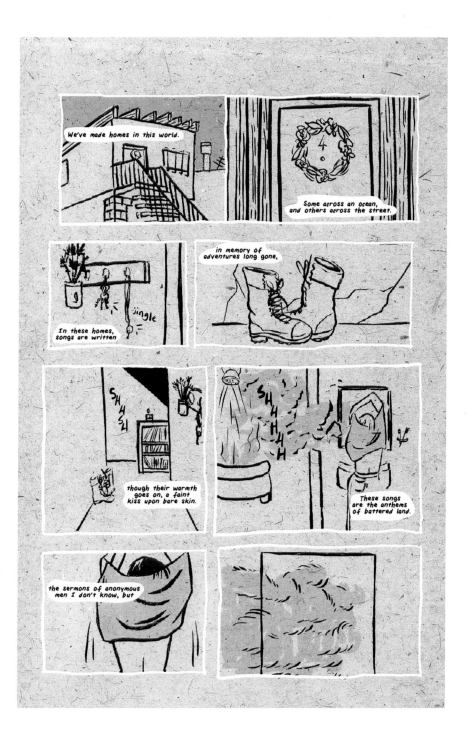

to the pinays
who have considered suicide

Caroline Calderon

Cast of Characters

Angel Lacson	Female. High School Age. Always rockin fresh kicks. Worships Lauryn Hill. Mr. Lacson's daughter.
Mr. Lacson	Male. Late 30's. Second Generation Filipino American. Divorced. Blue collar worker. Enjoys his hennessy. Angel's father.
JJ	Male. 16. Bopper.
School Kids	The audience to JJ's jokes
Commuters	SF residents who wait at the Balboa Park BART station every morning
Poster Boy	Male. Late Teens. Chose a better path.
Poster Woman	Female. 20's. Pinay. Survivor.
Lola	Female. Senior. Bag lady.

TIME

Present.

PLACE

San Francisco. The Lacson Family's living room and Balboa Park BART Station (a waiting place for commuters from various walks of life: techies, mothers, seniors, suits, uniforms, inner city youth; adorn with various ads about start ups, food, health, and other public service announcements)

> *Mr. Lacson is sitting on his favorite chair with his arms crossed, a glass of Hennessey rests on the end table beside him. He gets up, paces back and forth, stops. Wipes his face, thinks about how he is going to lay it down, and faces the audience.*

MR. LACSON

Was it worth it?

(pause)

MR. LACSON

You're not answering the question, I just want a yes or a no, was it worth it?

(he shakes his head)

MR. LACSON

And how many times did I warn you?

(pause)

I asked you a question…Ohh you acting like a little girl now, I thought you was a woman.

(MR. LACSON takes out his smart phone from his pocket, turns the camera towards the audience and hits record)

See this is what happens when you fuck up.

(MR. LACSON turns his camera phone to the ground)

All your beautiful hair gone because you didn't listen to me.

(He refocuses the camera to the audience)

What do you have to say for yourself?

(pause)

That's right and next time you're gonna listen to your daddy.

(He stops recording and puts the phone away. MR. LACSON reaches for his glass and takes a sip, wipes his mouth)

MR. LACSON
I am tired of this, you hear me? Clean this mess up and go to bed. You got school tomorrow.

(Blackout. Change scene)

It's Monday morning. SCHOOL KIDS are at the Balboa Park BART Station waiting for the Pittsburg/Baypoint Train before they head to school. The kids are goofing around when one decides to play Fetty Wap's "Trap Queen" on his portable speakers. The kids go wild when the song comes on. A man nearby irritated by the music puts his headphones on to listen to his "2014 Merengue Mix". The man takes a seat on the concrete bench next to a woman swiping up, up up, on her smartphone. ANGEL enters the scene with hoodie and backpack on. She notices the group of kids and her heart drops. She wasn't expecting to see them at the station. "9 car train arriving in five minutes" is announced through the station speakers. ANGEL puts on her headphones to drown out the sounds and people at the BART platform, all she can hear is Lauryn Hill's "That Thing."

ANGEL keeps her head down as she walks down the platform. The SCHOOL KIDS try to call out to ANGEL but she doesn't hear them. They start whispering, talking shit. One of them pulls out their phone, they all huddle to watch a video.

ANGEL is standing, tired and defeated. She is constantly fixing her hoodie. JJ starts walking towards Angel, the closer he gets the music fades from "That Thing" to "Trap Queen" in the background.

JJ

What's up Angel?

(ANGEL ignores JJ)

JJ

I know you can hear me. What, you too famous for me now?

> (JJ continues to talk with ANGEL but he cannot be heard by
> ANGEL nor the audience. The music switches, all they can
> hear is "That Thing". ANGEL takes a seat on the concrete
> bench. JJ tries waving at ANGEL but no response. ANGEL
> then leans forward from her seat, with her forehead buried in
> her hands and elbows on her lap. After many failed attempts
> to get ANGEL's attention, JJ decides to pull back ANGEL's
> hoodie and purposefully reveals ANGEL's humiliating haircut.
> Fade out background music)

JJ

Damn! Your dad really did make you cut off your hair.

> (ANGEL stands up immediately—frightened and humiliated,
> she is on the verge of crying.)

(screaming) Leave me alone!

> (All the people and sounds at the station freeze except ANGEL.
> She starts a spoken word piece.)

ANGEL

Weak. Disappointment. I refuse to be that girl
So I'm gonna to take one step forward, jump, I want out of this world
Hit the train hard and make this platform a yellow tape scene
Heart so heavy and scarred the coroner will announce, "she was only sixteen"
I mean who can blame the insane for wanting to end the pain?
It is my life and to go on would be living in vain
I just want to sleep on these tracks
Lay flat on my back, box me in, all dressed in black
I can't go back to the girl I used to be
I want to be free, what is it like to be free?
Was I ever free?

(There are two posters across from the concrete bench that ANGEL and the other commuters were sitting on. One poster displays a boy with the slogan "You are not alone". The other shows a picture of a woman with the slogan "Reach out. Save a life". Both posters come to life.)

POSTER BOY & POSTER WOMAN
(together) I understand your pain.

(POSTER BOY begins to tell his experience with suicide through spoken word and movement)

POSTER BOY

They say
it's your fault, your mistake
Useless.
They say stop making excuses
stop being a nuisance,
Little did they know my kuya was abusive

You see my brother
was always seeking comfort in women
but he actually never showed real comfort to a woman
ignorant of his own privilege
he sought comfort with me in my bed, despite my plea

because I was easy, speechless and broken
floatin' through life, feelings unspoken
no doctor could understand why I was so quiet
so tired, so depressed, so stupid
it was my fault, my mistake Useless.

o.d'd on the antidepressants that my psychiatrist prescribed to me
I thought it would be quick to quit being useless
When I woke up I saw the gates open from heaven
Several seconds later I realized no, this ain't heaven
my eyes were just burned by the fluorescents
I thought I was dead
but I was actually reborn
convalescent alive on a hospital bed

ANGEL

How did it feel?

POSTER BOY

What do you mean?

ANGEL

How did it feel to attempt suicide?

POSTER BOY

The pain I felt in that moment was not physical. My life was filled with broken fences I couldn't fix. With each pill I took, I thought I was one step closer to freedom.

ANGEL

That's what I want...to be free

POSTER BOY

You have a choice. Talk to someone. No one deserves to feel this way but there are people who can help.

ANGEL

You don't understand. The humiliation...

POSTER BOY

There is more to life than this hurt that you feel. Depression is not a choice, but suicide is. I made a choice but God gave me a second chance, not everyone is given the same fate. In the US, every 13 minutes there is one death by suicide... don't make my mistake, don't be another statistic

ANGEL

You think I want to be? Fuck your statistics. You don't know me, you don't know what I've been through. I have no one but myself.

POSTER BOY

That's not true. God is with you and he has a plan for you. Trust your struggle and Him to save you.

ANGEL

You've got to be kidding me. God save me? (laughs, ANGEL gets on her knees) God if you exist, please save me!

POSTER BOY

That's not what I meant. Just because I believe in God doesn't mean—

POSTER WOMAN
I tried to commit suicide at a police station.

(POSTER BOY and ANGEL look at each other confused)

POSTER WOMAN
I know it sounds crazy but my plan was to bring a toy gun into the station and then point it at a cop. You know, kill two birds with one stone. End my life, make a political statement.

ANGEL
How did it feel?

POSTER WOMAN
I actually didn't go through with it.

POSTER BOY
Why didn't you?

(POSTER WOMAN starts her spoken word piece.)

POSTER WOMAN
Silver tongued
his words left me rusted
Greedy with his midas touch, he got me frozen
his cold heart couldn't see that he was constantly killin' me
causing me to crash so willingly

My lover burned me third degree
and I was one hundred degrees, hot mess, reckless, didn't give a fuck
more or less, I must confess, I was done with the stress
I walked up the station steps
Knees weak, I crashed down and wept

I cried until I was able to breathe again
Inhaled all the possibilities
Exhaled all the self-hostility

ANGEL
How can I breathe when he has me trapped?

Caroline Calderon

ANGEL & POSTER WOMAN
To the pinays who have considered suicide

POSTER WOMAN
when the sun is enough
do not apologize for your brown skin
do not apologize for your smile
do not apologize for your tears
no one has the right to shame you for your trauma
no one has the right to tame you for your light

ANGEL
(to audience) Daddy you'll be sorry when I'm dead
But look at this way, you won't have to bring back bread
For this young bitch you fed

ANGEL & POSTER WOMAN
To the pinays who have considered suicide

POSTER WOMAN
when the sun is enough
believe in your ability
to make him really see
that you are unstoppable
and that freedom is possible.

His words will leave wounds that will eventually heal into scars
scars that you will carry but should not be ashamed of
people will try to destroy you
but your strongest defense is loving yourself
learn to love yourself.

ANGEL
But how? How do I love myself?

(singing) WHEN I LOOK INTO THE MIRROR I DON'T LIKE WHAT I SEE
PART OF ME IS GONE, I'M FEELING INCOMPLETE
OH WELL, SHOULD I LAY 6 FEET UNDER OR SHOULD I LIVE
THROUGH HELL
THEY SAY I'LL BE OKAY, EASIER SAID THAN DONE
WILL I LIVE TO SEE THE SUN?

POSTER WOMAN
(singing) I SAY YOU'LL FIND YOUR WAY
TOMORROW'S A NEW DAY
YOUR JOURNEY'S JUST BEGUN—

(The arrival of the upcoming BART train is announced.
Un freeze the commuters and kids. The ads are just ads.
ANGEL gets ready to jump in front of the oncoming train, a
snippet of "That Thing" echoes in the background, "watch out,
watch out". As the train approaches ANGEL takes several steps
forward. Enter LOLA with her granny cart who is in hurry to
catch the train. Just as ANGEL is about to jump, she is cut off
by LOLA who is apologetic for her bumping into ANGEL.)

LOLA
Excuse me anak! Ohhh no, why do you look so sad?

(LOLA hands ANGEL a stack of napkins from various fast
food restaurants she has hoarded)

Huwag kang umiyak. Then sun is shining, it's a beautiful day

ANGEL stands at the platform and watches LOLA,
the commuters and kids enter the train. She looks at her
stack of napkins, smirks, takes a deep breath and exhales.

BLACKOUT

W. Kyle Cudal De Ocera

Re-member

When you're depressed
Make sure you eat
Because you forget that
Everything comes back to normal,
Clock starts ticking again, and
Gravity remembers to put you back where you belong
Before everything caves in.

You ask what's wrong,
But mirrors never really answer back.
The face you see maybe the only chance at love you get.

Remember wanting to cry?
People say men don't
So you hold it in with guile and energy,
Severed roots, open wounds, phantom limb
Might jinx the future,
So you keep secrets from yourself
                    (You know you can never really leave)
Though you've always been a horrible liar
                    (You know there is nothing to come back to)
Though you're an addict at it,
                    (You've come far)
Just scared once heart make up its mind

You forget,
The world obeys,
Accept it,

Cook yourself a nice meal,
And try to get some sleep
Before breakfast
Because you're going to need
All the courage
You have
To make it
Back

SALVADOR VELASCO

Panahon

Reptiles in glass cages litter all ends of the room. A cat with a head twice the size of a fist sleeps on the top bunk of a bed. A TV on its stand, an unused ab roller, and one of the many cages inhabited by one of the many reptiles hinders a walk in closet. As she enters the room, all turn a quick welcoming and knowing stare. With her in the middle, the four walls are complete. Returning from the life outside, she succumbs to her domain. Her things fall to different corners of the floor, winding herself down to exactly how she left every thing- still in its place. Her shoes come off, followed by her socks. Barefoot, she leaves for the kitchen to peer into the cluttered fridge, only to go back empty handed. The sudden shock of the kitchen's linoleum leaves her body as she feels the warmth of the carpet.

"There'll be time enough for feeding. I wasn't hungry anyway,"
She convinces herself.

Overspent, she slides into the lower bunk of her bed, still in her day clothes.
She pulls the blanket over her head and wishes for sleep to come quickly.
Minutes pass.
She tosses and turns hoping for the mattress to comfort her.
As her eyes fail to grow heavy,
as the moon travels from one end of the night sky to the other,
she finds herself letting go,
once again crying herself
finally to sleep.

A Big Bowl of Julia

Julia Holt

While growing up, I always thought I knew who I was and where I came from. My name is Julia Holt, and as a child, I was always told that I should be happy with what I was given. But I grew up and found out that I was cursed.

I was born in America but my ethnicity is Filipino. I grew up with the big spoon and fork hanging on my dining room wall; the twelve apostles securely on my door frame; and adobo with rice for breakfast, lunch, dinner, and snack. I never had to study my Filipino culture; it came naturally for me because I was surrounded by it. Being Filipino in my family meant also being Catholic; there was not a single person in my family who was not Catholic. From age five to twelve. I attended a private catholic school. We studied the Bible, went to church as a school, and learned about God. At home, this religion was also implemented. There was a small altar next to my room where I prayed the rosary every night, my family prayed before every meal, and we went to church every Sunday. While growing up, all my faith, hope, and dreams were put into God and prayers. I soon realized I had to stop relying on God for my hopes and dreams to come true.

I was two when my mom died. My aunt and uncle adopted my siblings and I and we moved to San Jose. When I was twelve, my dad died. When I was 17, I became depressed. My siblings, both older than me, moved out of the house and their relationship between my fill-in-parents, just as mine, was non-existent. Growing up my relationship with my aunt and uncle grew thinner and thinner. I was constantly reminded that I was a burden and that they were doing me a favor since they adopted me after the death of both my parents. I prayed and prayed to just be happy, to not cry on my birthday, to enjoy Christmas, to not feel worthless, and to enjoy just one day but nothing ever happened. I felt my life was a waste. In that moment, I knew that in order for me to be happy, I had to want to be happy. I stopped praying and found a way to be happy. I was still 17 when I graduated high school, and four days after graduation, I moved out. Moving out pulled me out of my prolonged depression. I pulled away from drugs and isolation and picked myself up. I reintroduced myself to one of my favorite hobbies—sports. I even found out that one of my hidden identities was an adrenaline junky, which is why I've loved sports since I was a child. Sports made my heart pump, my senses alerted, and made me feel good. I even picked up sports like rock climbing and river rafting. I was happy.

The first 17 years of my life were not the most joyous, but without those first 17 years, I would not be who I am today. I know my experiences aren't the most typical childhood stories and they are not ones that I dwell on often. However, the past is the past, and I can not change what has happened nor would I want to. Those events are what make me--me. As a child, I was always told I was happy with what I was given. But I grew up and found out that I could not be given happiness, I had to want it in order to achieve it.

Eileen R. Tabios

From "The Gilded Age of Kickstarters"

There Was the First Vegetal Cyborg

89 backers
$5,448
pledged of $55,183 goal
22 days to go

Cities encroach

Gentle them with house plants

But not everyone has a green thumb

The French come to the rescue
with "Still Human"

a company with a smart flowerpot

The pot alerts humans
to a plant's needs

    does it need water?
    does it need light?
    does it need fertilizer?
    does it need heat or to cool down?

Designed to sit atop railings
it may have the added benefit
of dissuading suicide
in the concrete jungle

Named "Biom" for an ecosystem
it offers a new vision

        of our street
        of our building
        of our landscape
        of our life

The path to decolonization
requires nature

Sinangag and Tostones in West Harlem

Leah K. Sicat

When I think of home, I think of cha-cha music, lumpia, and pancit at family parties in California and pinsan sleepovers and sinangag brunches around the dining table the following morning. Swaying to the rhythm of bachata music at the beginners dance class one Friday night brought all those memories back to me as the dance instructor asked the students to note how "tropical-y" and slow the music sounded. At first, I struggled with why bachata brought a rush of memories in that brief moment listening for the beat. The breezy, relaxing tempo took me back to my years living in West Harlem fresh out of college, grappling with the absurdity and raw resilience of diaspora and shared histories and knowledges.

During late weekday afternoons, with the crowded subway stations and everyday commuters crammed into a single car, I used to look forward to transferring from the A train to the Uptown 1 train headed home to West Harlem. When Jay-Z mentions Dominicanos, Harlem, Broadway, and that McDonald's, I know which neighborhood he's talking about. Not to imply this particular place became familiar beyond measure, there was something unintentionally residual and simultaneously foreign about how people of diaspora, embodiments of colonial legacies and a U.S. imperial present, coincide and respond amidst colliding factors that bring us together. New York City, after the invasion of Iraq and before the 2008 market crash, was an interesting time and place. I had just moved there from California as a new young teacher, grappling with how my class, gender, ethnicity, compounded migration, and heritage represented gentrification in the neighborhood with the cheapest possible apartment that I could afford.

One afternoon visiting a cafe in my neighborhood, a young waiter who had been conversing with me leaned in and asked how come some Filipinos have Spanish last names. I responded, "The same reason you do." He paused, looked bewildered for a moment, and nodded. That particular instance stays with me precisely because asking questions is necessary and so is an understanding of history. What would we do without the understanding and questioning of what has happened? Or, rather, what can we do without an understanding of shared histories and the active participation of those who share it with us? Even when we don't immediately see shared connections and valuable differences, at what point can our shared experiences, histories, and intergenerational traumas shape possibilities for conversations and paths moving forward?

I don't have any answers. Just questions and lots of reading to do. Hopefully, not alone. And importantly, not just for my own benefit. There will be memories and associations that just don't seem to make sense but unexpectedly come up anyway particularly while hearing cha-cha and bachata and eating tostones, arroz con gandules, lumpia, and pancit canton.

Waking up to the sounds of bachata music and seeing vendors sell jicama and plantains in cardboard boxes on the street is the background for how I learned to cook Filipino food. New York City isn't the city where I grew up, but it's the place where I grew. Living on my own for the first time, I learned to appreciate cafe con leche from the corner bodega for my early morning commute and fried cheese and mangu for an occasional weekend breakfast. I also learned how far creativity, with an attempt for integrity, could go and how delicious it could be.

Audre Lorde notes: "Survival isn't some theory operating in a vacuum. It's a matter of my everyday living and making decisions." Survival happens everyday in classrooms, in the streets, and in the kitchen. When I think of how I learned to cook, my memory goes back to the times of cooking in my tiny West Harlem apartment. Figuring out over that little stove how to fry lumpia—the way my parents did—and tostones—like the ones I got down the block—in the same sizzling hot oil. Lumpia, the crunchy hand-held rolled envelopes of tender chicken and vegetables. Tostones, the green platanos sold on the city sidewalks of my predominantly Dominican neighborhood that I learned how to fry and smash and fry again. Rich with flavor, they perfectly complimented sinangag, the garlic fried rice that I learned to love. Steak, sinangag, and tostones became my favorite dish to cook when friends visited. It was my way of sharing the foods I enjoyed out of the ingredients that were available. They were my form of transnational cooking, survival, and nourishment.

This reflection on cooking is not about mere consumption. It's not about merely ingesting what can be bought, but how to create, cook up, or remix circumstances that we encounter and how to sustain ourselves and each other. How do we build within and across collective struggles against the legacies of colonialism and imperialism? How do we protest or perpetuate patriarchy, white supremacy, and imperialism in our everyday lives? At what point do certain differences become trivial? And, let's not forget about amplifying the voices of those most impacted. At the same time, what are the creative and critical combinations we cook up for sustenance, nourishment, and ongoing education?

Too Funky for White People: Filipino Recipes and Inauthenticity in Dale Talde's Asian-American Cookbook

JONATHAN A. VALDEZ

University of Hawaiʻi at Mānoa

When I came back from my first trip to the Philippines in 2008, a distinct event happened in the Los Angeles International Airport baggage claim that showed me the power of Filipino food. As my father and I were waiting for our luggage amidst the sea of suitcases and balikbayan boxes an overpowering and pungent smell began to overtake the baggage claim area. As the smell of fermented fish wafted through the air, many Filipino faces in the crowd refused to reveal any emotion as a certain realization began to set in. That realization was that their prized possession of bagoong had shattered. The smell caught the attention of many non-Filipinos in the area. A group of Korean exchange students was excited by the familiar smell of fermented fish while a junior TSA officer began pacing around, worried that a terrorist attack was happening. The officer's anxiety was finally relieved when his senior officer calmly handed him a bottle of Febreze and told him to go track down the box with the broken bagoong bottle.

I use this anecdote to show how a staple ingredient of Filipino cuisine is full of controversy and promise in the Filipino and American imagination. On one hand, bagoong is a symbol of home-style cooking in the Philippines where it invokes the nostalgia of home and serves as a symbol and ingredient of authenticity. Alternatively, bagoong symbolized second

74

generation Filipino American kids' sense of difference who did not know how to cope or explain their parent's ethnic cuisine. In this paper I explore how Chef Dale Talde, a second generation Filipino American discusses bagoong, ideas of authenticity and inauthenticity in his cooking and how Filipino food reveals stories of immigration, alienation, and desires of returning home to the Philippines through his cookbook *Asian-American: Proudly Inauthentic Recipes from the Philippines to Brooklyn*.

Talde was born in 1978 and raised by first generation Filipino immigrant parents in Chicago. In the introduction of *Asian-American*, Talde opens the book recounting how his mother always kept a pig's head in the oven in case they ever had company over. The candid and brash introduction sets up the rest of *Asian-American* as part cookbook and part biography. For Talde, cooking with inauthenticity is a reflection of his life growing up in the United States, but more importantly, it serves as a critique of what we consider ethnic Filipino cuisine. I examine how two recipes in Asian-American that Talde labels with an advisory notice to readers of their explicit Filipino-ness are critiques of the Filipino experience in the United States.

The smell and taste of Filipino food can trigger Filipino immigrants' memories and evoke a feeling of being home in the Philippines. Filipino cuisine for many people can transport people back to the Philippines without being there physically. While this sense of authenticity may stimulate good memories of home, recipes that use authentic ingredients can also remind immigrants of their unsavory experiences of poverty and hardship in the Philippines.[1] What makes Talde's appeal for inauthenticity in Asian American cuisine interesting because it pushes back against the western, commodified expectations of Asian cuisine in the United States while also accounting for the Filipino immigrant experience. Martin Manalansan argues that inauthenticity needs to be seen "not as a lack of authentic elements (whatever they may be) but as a historically and cultural negotiated state and process of emotional discomfort and affective refusal to adhere to a straightforward mapping of identity. In other words...inauthenticity is a

---

[1] For more of a discussion on this please read Martin Manalansan's "Beyond Authenticity: Rerouting the Filipino Culinary Diaspora" in *Eating Asian American: A Food Studies Reader.*

way to break apart the static notions of "Filipino-ness" by refusing to obey its strictures and clichés of food and identity".[2] For Talde, inauthenticity is the ethos of his cookery. By subscribing to inauthenticity as his cooking philosophy, Talde expresses this economically through his choices in cooking and also through how he views the recipe's personal connection to himself. The ability to adapt and try to recreate the flavors of home sees Filipino culinary inauthenticity as acts of survival in the Filipino diaspora.

Talde asks "what's so bad about being inauthentic?".[3] To Talde, this proverbial "what's authentic rabbit hole" reveals the vast diasporic nature of food and shows that authenticity is not so static. Particularly, thinking about Filipino food, inauthenticity shows the longstanding colonial and imperial influence still existing in our dishes. The Spanish and American influence on ingredients such as olives, raisins, and items like cacao show how ingredients traveled between Europe, North America, and the Philippines and became a part of the Filipino imagination of high-class food. Thus, when we think about foods like champorado or longanisa as inauthentic we connect how the history and taste of colonialism and diaspora became real for our parents. By looking into the inauthenticity of Filipino food, we can look into the ways are parents sought to recreate flavors by searching out familiar ingredients. When they were unable to do so, they substituted ingredients that could serve their taste memories and brought them back to their memories of the Philippines.

Talde runs counter to Manalansan, who argues that food brings people back to the Philippines. Alternatively, Talde cooks for the opposite reason stating that "My food is meant to remind you that you're home, in that strange and awesome country where we live".[4] For Talde, home is not in the Philippines but the United States. Talde came of age in the mid-1990s and cut his teeth as a chef in the 2000s which influenced his cooking to push against the essentialization of Asian cuisines and culture often seen in restaurants featuring Asian concepts in their menu. While restaurants such as Pok Pok run by chef Andy Ricker seek to transport the diner to

---

[2] Ku 297, author's emphasis
[3] Talde 43
[4] Talde 19

northern, rural Thailand, Talde's ambition to redefine and reimagine Asian and especially Filipino cuisine reveals his agency in pushing back against the essentialist scripts of what should be in Asian food.

The push back against essentialization comes from the usage of ingredients in recipes. With the proliferation of ethnic Asian supermarkets, the importation of Asian ingredients became more accessible to American consumers. Talde discusses the lack of a key ingredient in his mother's recipes, bagoong. The lack of ingredients like bagoong symbolized a lack of authenticity since a signature component of the food's flavor was missing. However, Talde recounts how his mother prepared her sofrito, a Spanish vegetable sauce mixed with fried, canned sardines as a substitute to bagoong. This makeshift fish sauce served to satisfy the memory of Talde's mother and father who sought to keep Filipino food in their families' lives. Talde's mom preparing sofrito is but one of the many ways Filipino parents attempted to feed Filipino food to their families without all of the ingredients. The inauthenticity of her recipe is bound by their family living in the Midwest and the economic and geographic barriers to acquiring "authentic" ingredients.

Amidst the challenge of access to ingredients, Filipino immigrant parents also faced issues of time working long hours to support their families. A major reason that Talde says inauthenticity is key to his recipes is to reduce the amount of time spent in the kitchen brings you closer to family. Talde says to buy cooked rice at a market or using a cheap sauce or alternative ingredients to rethink how much time we commit to cooking. It also shows how Talde himself is thinking about the economic sense of restaurants, home cooking, and the economic time of Filipino families. Not everyone has access to specific ingredients, so Talde calls for people to take the cheapest and easiest route to ensure more time is spent with friends and family. The work the first generation took to provide for their family took massive tolls on immigrant families. *Asian-American* thus is also a call for younger generations who may have a more comfortable relationship to food to consider that the time shared eating the food is much more important that making everything from scratch.

Talde discusses how his beef Kare-Kare and the green mango salad are "too funky for white people" despite his modern take on the two dishes. The common ingredient between both is bagoong or the Sofrito recipe listed in *Asian-American*. Connecting the Kare-Kare recipe to memories spent with family during Christmas time transports Talde to memories of being with family in Chicago. Similarly, the green mango salad recipe is an adaption from the simple snack he used to share with his grandmother, Lola Cresenciana, of ripe green mango smothered with bagoong. The combination of flavors sour, salty, and what Talde describes as "funky" demonstrates how the traditional preparations and his inauthentic takes on the two dishes are considered alien and non-palatable by his New York City customers.

The reimagined nature of Talde's recipes disrupts the white diners search for authentic Filipino flavors and their desire to experience the exotic. For these two dishes, both are plated aesthetically for individual diners as opposed to the large communal, family bowl. Talde's Kare-Kare is also made with beef short ribs as opposed to ox-tail and marrow pieces. By using more expensive cuts of beef rather than the cheap cuts used in the traditional recipe, Talde seeks to bridge Filipino food to the mainstream audiences using cuts found in other American eateries. Keeping true to the easily sourced ingredients he calls for smooth peanut butter you could easily buy at a supermarket but also adds Thai chili peppers to the recipe. This inauthentic ingredient sourcing and additions demonstrate how Talde positions Kare-Kare, as something akin to a Thai or Indian curry.

This similarity to Thai food is also apparent in the plating for the green mango salad; Talde prepares it similarly to Som Tam, the Thai green papaya salad. Talde displays a level of pride that he got the recipe and flavors right by stating that this is the dish at his restaurant Talde that gets sent back the most to the kitchen. Perhaps being the funkiest of his recipes, Talde's Spicy Green Mango Salad, features bagoong but also features nontraditional ingredients such as coconut flakes, chili peppers, and shallots. The striking feature of this recipe is that by the dish being sent back to the kitchen, it signals just how the funkiness of the dish is an alienable aspect of the dish. The tart, spicy, and funkiness of the entire dish shows how both Talde's sensibilities towards authenticity and inauthenticity are refused by his customers. The refusal of the funky dish also demonstrates how American perceptions of Filipino food. When customers return the spicy mango salad back to the kitchen shows how a recipe catered to the western palette is refused because its flavors are not palatable to the American tongue.

Talde's funkiness is of bagoong and the Filipino recipes that use it reminds us that both Filipino food and people are still exoticized and alienated from main street America. What Talde demonstrates through the irreverent and unapologetic inauthenticity of his Filipino or Asian recipes is that it defies western, and Eurocentric ideas of what the Philippines is. The funkiness of Talde's recipes and their usage of bagoong reminds us that it the difference and non-sensibilities of the immigrant experience that influence Talde to cook inauthentically. Cooking inauthentic food should not be seen as breaking the rules of Filipinoness, but rather asserting the many different identities and histories that make Filipino and Filipino American food what it is today.

WORKS CITED

Manalansan, Martin. 2013. "Beyond Authenticity: Rerouting the Filipino Culinary Diaspora." In *Eating Asian America: A Food Studies Reader*, by Robert Ji-Song Ku, Martin F. Manalansan and Anita Mannur, 288-302. New York: New York University Press.

Talde, Dale, and J.J. Goode. 2015. *Asian-American: Proudly Inauthentic Recipes from the Brooklyn to Brooklyn*. New York: Grand Central Life & Style.

SUTURING OUR SPLIT SELVES:
ON INTERSECTIONALITY

Trish Guevarra

Beneath My Maria Clara

I love my Maria Clara.

tattered and dirtied by pain
that brought me to my knees
rosaries in hand
beads stitched by your hands
touched by his hands
demeaned by this man.

but, I still love my Maria Clara.

wrapped in pinya
terno dresses
beneath are her secrets
betel nut tucked
prayers chanted

her spirit is still there

Beneath my Maria Clara.

DOMINIQUE DEFOE

Living Within The Cusp

My peers take pride in the fact that they don't see color, but I know I do. I grew up with the world at my fingertips; watching the colors of cultures swirl around me in billowing skirts and lacy fans, listening to the hums of lullabies from places I could pronounce before I knew my own name, and learning historical truths from those who lived through them. I am a cultural fusion. The product of two immigrant children from two different oceans who came to America on the curtails of hope, though they still trail coconuts, cliffs, islands, and revolutions on the ground they walk on. These are the footsteps that I followed, and living within the cusp of vivid cultures and having an identity that is so often ridiculed, appropriated, and then tossed aside has driven me to become a voice for oppression of all kinds.

I am different because I am shameless, and unafraid.

Age twelve; arguing with my dad and his friends that love is love. Age thirteen; responding to comments that I was so lucky to be a 'golden shade', to have 'good hair', and to not have a 'black nose' by coming back the next school year four shades darker. Age fourteen; delving into the thoughts of Malcolm X, Bell Hooks, and Maya Angelou. Age fifteen; performing in a poetry slam with a piece comparing the destruction of Mother Nature to the the destruction of women themselves. Age sixteen; becoming aware of and attempting to correct my own biases. I am different because my entire life has been a huge opportunity, I have had the privilege of being surrounded by living relics of history who have taken care to reiterate their knowledge and stories to me, no matter how painful. In their lives they battled physical restraints, in mine, I address those which are ingrained, and, because of my family, I am not afraid.

My existence is the personification of the messy American dream—a swirl of intersectionality. One of the first things I remember from my childhood is the questions. "What are you?" "She is so beautiful, what is she mixed with?" All of this was in my realm of comfort until I was thirteen and meeting a friend's mom for the first time. While attempting to introduce myself I was interrupted with one of the questions, after politely motoring off the bones of my ancestry she eyed me up and down, winked at her seventeen year old son, and said, "How exotic," at which he smiled. In that moment I felt every bit a curiosity, nothing but a token of both the dragons of the East and the sweltering sun of the islands, more alien than human. I still remember the feeling of burning, the realization that people's fascination rested not on who I was, but what I was.

My name is Dominique. Dominique. Dominique. Dominique.

For months after, explaining my heritage felt less like pride and more like spilling my blood onto kitchen floors, extracting my soul and exposing my lifeline to people who felt it was owed to them. Then, I stammered my way through, struggling to encapsulate my culture in a few sentences, ever aware of my unfamiliarity. But now, sixteen, with fire replacing hesitance and confidence overtaking tolerance, this is my answer:

I am a black filipina woman, and I am proud.

My dance teacher has always described me as a burst, explosions occurring with every step I take. I move to a different rhythm, leaving hurricanes in my wake. When I dance, I feel my history. Knowledge that extends far beyond my birth, instinctive flair and stylistic movements that are more inherent than learned. I hear the soft whistles of wind weaving through sugar cane, of cries for revolution echoing in abandoned villages, of ships leaving port in tune to the rattling of silver chains. I feel the dirt rising from the pounding of brown toes which is then lost in the tangles of curly hair. I feel the blood. I feel the tears. I feel the joy. The most profound connections I have ever experienced are with people who are long dead.

Decades from now I hope for my descendants to hear my truth as loudly as I have heard those that came before me. I hope that shouts for justice rattle through their teeth as they do through mine. I hope that the legacy of culture runs through their veins at the same speed which it courses through me. But most of all, I hope that one day they will hear the true bells of freedom ringing.

Blacknpinay is…

Teresa Hodges

Blacknpinay is…

Mindin' My Own Business Then Makin' It My Business

When I was on the Daly City bus minding my own business with my tote bag that was made to look like a huge Filipino flag, a Filipina auntie barked at me, "you are patronizing our culture." I was shocked that she was so forwardly accusatory. I was so shocked that it took me awhile to find my voice until I finally responded to her in Tagalog politely so that it would save face. Afterwards I thought why was I trying to help HER save face? I realized I wasn't trying to make enemies but instead, seeking that Filipina/o community in Daly City that I experienced in Daly City elsewhere like with the cashiers at Walgreens or clerk at Trader Joes who always spoke Tagalog to me. She responded more softly but hesitantly saying, why do you speak Tagalog?, a question that I usually get when Filipinas/os find out I speak some Tagalog. So I told her I am Black and Filipina, my mom is Pinay. And she was like OH and proceeded to talk to me like everything was fine. Whenever people say or do messed up things to me, I sometimes never respond to them, often only thinking of something to say hours later and once I've left the scene of oppression. But in this instance, it reminds me that when I feel strong in who I am, I felt strong enough to speak my truths. For me, embracing my identity and cultures as blacknpinay helps me know my worth and that I come from strong people. It means that I can ask my ancestors to give me strength, as my friends remind me, especially during times when I don't know what to do. Blacknpinay means strength because when I am faced with people that think being Black is inferior and that Filipinas are all submissive and obedient, I have friends and family that show and remind me otherwise. Whenever things go down and it is safe for me to do so, I have the choice—not obligation, but depending on the situations, my choice—to be responsible and tell folks when something isn't right, not just for the sake of my feelings but also all the other blacknpinays and blacknpinoys. Blacknpinay is a commitment to myself to be true and real to myself and to others.

Embracing Many, Even Opposing, Truths

I am Black. People see me and they usually think I am *only* Black, even with my long curly hair and hazel eyes. They often think I have "good hair" but still Black. I am Filipina. I call myself the secret Asian sometimes because even when I say so, people don't always think I am Filipina. Even though my parents have been together for almost 40 years, my mom was the one that took care of us mostly. I have lot of influence from her culturally even though strangers do not think we're related when we're standing at the grocery store line together. Once at Trader Joe's, my mom and I were at the register speaking Tagalog and the cashier was staring at us like he was trying to figure it out, barely looking at the items he was scanning. I am a woman. For me, "Pinay" indicates that I am also a strong Filipina woman. Being Black and Filipina/Pinay are categories on it's own, as well as ways in which being Black is influenced by my being Pinay and being Pinay is influenced by my being Black. For example, I lived in the Philippines for a year while in college and people would tell me "talagang Pilipino ka," you are really/truly Filipino. However, I also feel comfortable around Black people and visiting my family in the South. Yet at the same time, I know that since people look at me and tend to perceive me as Black, I do not experience being Filipina through appearance the same way that people that "look Filipina/o" are treated based on their appearance. So, to call myself blacknpinay enables me to not only embody but be perceived as someone who is Black, Filipina, and mixed race and therefore expand notions of what it means to look Filipina. Naming myself blacknpinay makes me proud to be Black and Filipina and envelopes my various essences. It is significant for me that I embrace a word that encompasses a mixed, but critically conscious identity, and word that encompasses blackness and Filipinaness, and womanness, but it doesn't mean that every mixed person has to identify as mixed, nor do I push a mixed identity ALL the time. But perhaps what matters more is what blacknpinay represents to me.

Community Accepting and Keeping it Real With You, Then Holding You Accountable

It was in my Filipina/o American community of Pin@y Educational Partnerships, PEP, where the word blacknpinay was nurtured. My good friend Artistel would always talk about me "keepin it blacknpinay" and remind me to be true to myself. My sister-friend Edeline's phone would autocorrect "blacknpinay" when she started typing bl... and despite the excitement of this, she reminds me to stay humble. My sister-friend Geraldine who took photos of me as part of her and friend Pauline's Natural Beauty Project and really made me see the beauty in blacknpinay. Manang Arlene would always greet me, "wuz up, blacknpinay?" and would always keep it real with me. My good-friend Raju, Indipino, who would (and still does) call me out and always push me to do and be better because I am blacknpinay. My good-friend Rhommel constantly reminds me that I'm blacknpinay and therefore strong and able to do whatever I want. In PEP there was all of that and so much more. It was with PEP folks that I got my blacknpinay tattoo, it was while a graduate student at SFSU that PEP Director Professor Ate Allyson Tintiangco-Cubales (along with Professor Wei Ming Dariotis) always encouraged me to write my Master's thesis on what I really wanted to write about—mixed blacknpinays, it was in PEP that so many people called me blacknpinay that the word was a normal word in our organization of about 60 people and everyone knew what it meant. I had felt for a long time that it was accepted for me to be Filipina, there wasn't an issue about that— especially here. However sometimes other Filipinas/os look down on my Blackness and don't like Black people in general and it tends to be obvious to me when I encounter people like that. Ironically it was in this community, a Filipina/o focused community, that I knew it was ok to really be Black in a Filipina/o American space. PEP counters antiblackness. PEP not only embraced my Blackness, not only encouraged my Blackness, but it encouraged me to learn more about that aspect of my identity and culture and further feel more comfortable about investing/committing to the betterment of that community. Being blacknpinay in this largely Filipina/o space helped me also to be Black. This is not to say that I didn't want to be Filipina, but I already knew I could be Filipina, and I already knew I could be mixed too. But here…I knew it was ok that a Filipina is also Black.

When Haters Hate, Gotta Re-Educate

Some people have asked me "why is it always about blacknpinay? Blacknpinay this and that…" And someone else asked me why it is always about race. What they didn't know is that growing up I felt a shame being Black because of the way society feels about Black people, and I also felt alienated from Filipino culture, i.e. not knowing either my mom's language of Cebuano or Tagalog. In college, I felt the pressure more that people saw me as Black and not as Filipina, because growing up I was always around my mom and aunties so I knew I was also Filipina. In addition, considering the oppression of and racism against Black and Filipin@ peoples, how do I see myself also as a human who is Black and Filipina and therefore also worthy of love and respect? Blacknpinay is not just political, it is also emotional and spiritual. I used to fight with my hair, all big and curly; I used to clothespin my nose some nights hoping it would get thinner. I used to try to talk pleasantly and not be controversial as a Filipina and not be threatening as a Black woman. I came into an understanding of what it means to be Black and what it means to be Filipina, in terms of my own relationship to those words and cultures and people, and finally found homes within it. Thus for me, blacknpinay means overcoming.

Possibilities

There is something that I learn from my experiences of "keepin it blacknpinay": it takes constant deliberate effort to learn what those identities and heritages mean to me—it is work. So to be blacknpinay means a culmination of everything that I talked about into a new expression of possibilities. While not everyone is Blacknpinay, the process of being Pin@y still engages elements of speaking your truths; embracing many, even opposing, truths; community/acceptance/accountability; re-educating haters; and possibilities. And when Pin@ys accept blacknpinays and Mexipinas and Indipinos, we not only resist anti-blackness/Mexicanness/ Indianness, etc, but we nurture communities that embrace blackness/ Mexicanness/Indianness which doesn't always happen in Pin@y communities.

Blacknpinay is about community but not entirely. Naming blacknpinay gives me the confidence to stand up even when my community isn't physically around. It gives me the strength to know that I am loved, accepted, and wanted, that I matter. It isn't specifically just that it is the word blacknpinay that does that, but it is also the sentiment, the meaning and process of me affirming myself, my communities affirming me, and also affirming our relationship to one another. Blacknpinay is love for myself, love for my people, and love for the world.

What you just call me??!! Challenging Forced Labels on Filipin@s of Mixed Heritage

MAHARAJ "RAJU" DESAI

It was a chilly December night in 2015 in San Bruno. I was sitting there in the theater, next to my friend Lulu, watching the Tagalog comedy "Beauty and the Bestie." As I sat there munching on popcorn, watching a scene about a queer beauty pageant, a contestant in ragged clothing came on the screen. The pageant host then said, "*Mukha kang bumbay,*" which translated literally means you look like an Indian (from India). However, the subtitles read "You look like a money lender." This is a stereotype that I and many of my family members have grown up hearing all our lives. We are mixed-heritage Indian and Filipin@s. Bumbay was a word that we all grew up hearing on a regular basis, even those of us that were born and raised in California. It always seemed like bumbay always meant something "other" both un-Filipin@ and un-American. It felt like a word that meant foreign, alien, inferior, savage, and even ugly all at the same time.

According to the UP Diksiyonaryong Pilipino (2010 edition), bumbay means the following:

1. a variety of onion (i.e. shallot)
2. a male goat

Meanwhile, the word Indian means:

1. citizen or native of India
2. Native American from a tribe/nation of America or the Caribbean
3. Anything about India, American Indians, or Native Indian

Some speculate that Bumbay was used to describe the turbans that Sikh men wore which looked similar to shallots. While others claim that the term Bumbay originally was the word Bombay pronounced with a Filipino accent and was used to refer to people from India. Either way, it has since been officially changed to Indian and there is no "official" connection of the word bumbay to Indian people. However, there are still so many really ugly and negative stereotypes associated with that word that remain. In our own home we were often teased by our own relatives for looking or being the most bumbay. It wasn't until I got older that I learned the connotation of bumbay to the term 5/6 or moneylender because of the way Indians in the Philippines were stereotyped as moneylenders. In fact, in my first time working with an all Tagalog-speaking Ethnic Studies lunchtime group at a local high school, I was frequently referred to as 5/6 by some of the youth I worked with.

Fortunately for me, it was also during that same time period that a good friend of mine who is also of mixed-heritage taught me the importance of naming yourself. She had found the term Blacknpinay as a way for her to define herself and her experiences as a Black and Filipin@ American woman. She gave me a shirt with the word Indipino written on it. It was incredible—suddenly, I no longer had to always explain myself and justify my existence to people. By having my own term, I no longer needed to validate my existence. I need to point out that it is not just people of Indian/Pakistani and Filipin@ mixed heritage that use this term. This term has also been used by people of Native American and Filipino mixed heritage. There is something powerful about being able to name and define yourself on your own terms.

Recently over the past year, I had the opportunity to present and write a book chapter on Indipin@s. As part of the process, I interviewed some of the only other Indipin@s I know—four of my cousins. Initially, this was an awkward and uncomfortable process because we never really talk about race/ethnicity, mixed heritage, or identity in a serious way in our family. I was used to only having these types of conversations in school in my Ethnic Studies classes and among my peers and friends. I didn't know which way these conversations would go and how my family would take them. I wasn't even sure how to ask certain questions. In the end, it was good process and I was really surprised that many of us shared similar experiences of being teased both inside our family, but also outside by people in our schools and communities—both here in America and in the Philippines as well. I was also surprised to hear that they were all always seen as an ethnicity other than their own—usually called Latina or Samoan by classmates and co-workers. It was really interesting for me to actually hear their stories. The interviews seemed a little difficult to do at times because they were often surprised by my questions and didn't know how to respond. I think this may have been the first time that someone may have asked them how they felt about their identity. I hope that the process was useful for them and helped them begin to process and heal from some of the ways that their identities were defined and/or denied by other people. I know that was definitely true for me.

The same year that I was writing that book chapter, I presented at a very large and popular Filipin@ American conference in San Diego with my colleagues from Hawai'i. After our presentation, I was heckled by an audience member who questioned the validity of my research and my identity by saying that "You are not even a Filipino. How are you a Filipino?" A few years ago, something like this would have shaken me to my core. I remember an incident in high school where a so-called "friend" of mine was questioning my identity behind my back. Back then, the way I "dealt" with that confrontation was to just avoid interactions with Filipin@s outside of my family and close social circle. That's not the way I reacted in San Diego. Instead, this time, I was able to politely reject her claim of authority over Filipin@-ness and realize that her discomfort/apprehension towards me was more a reflection of her own insecurities and really had more to do with her than me. Had I thought of it in the moment, I might have said, "Maybe I'm not 100% Filipin@, but I'm 100% Indipin@."

Overall, the process of learning about Critical Mixed Race Studies and the importance for people of mixed heritage to name and define themselves has really helped me feel more comfortable and confident with my mixed identity. I have begun to fully embrace both sides of my identity and don't have a need to quantify my different heritages based on other people's expectations such as appearance, blood quantum, or the ability to speak either language. I currently teach Filipino (Tagalog) and am a student of

Hindi language at the University of Hawai'i at Mānoa. In both spaces people initially expect the opposite of me—to be a student in the Filipino classroom and a teacher or expert in the Hindi classroom because of what I look like. If not for this long process of coming to terms with my identity as an Indipin@ and the process of owning that name, I would not have been able to overcome and continue to thrive in these spaces. I think this is a very important process for Filipin@s of mixed heritage to do—to find and name their communities in order to build, heal, and grow.

Losing Sampaguita

KAREN MARIE MALIWAT VILLA

Where is it?
Where was it?
Where did it go?

This journey
This road
I can recall how your ears look this thing that is
was real
no sense no time spent enough only time to time
where is this road
was it where I went?
into the dark
a sense of innocence
and resent the restlessness
I spent
where is where I went?
came back from
call upon, unearth
unbirth
pestilence
a pest where I went
this innocence was part of it a part of me
my fingers tie a knot
this is…
this is…
this is what I forgot

At home on tv, I would go to Mr. Roger's house or Pee Wee's Play-house. So many friends, so many neighbors. The legos would hurt my feet on the carpet. Poking me in my toes. The star-shaped metal jacks would imprint themselves too. But this adult house, this cold dark house with the curtains drawn and a white transparent one underneath covered the only window. The house was empty. Toyless. Friendless. No neighbors. He was alone in this house and maybe I was his toy, some light from an-other place that he could play with. Tell his stories to. We pretended to take showers. This was a game. But games have rules, a winner. Like four-square, or tetherball. I couldn't figure out what the goal was. How to "win." This touching and laying and showering.

The next day, I was walking to school with Angeline. It was only a couple blocks. She was chubby, always courteous. She dressed so well and her t-shirt or tops would be tucked in so neatly. I remember thinking, "She doesn't wear Bugle Boys like me." She didn't have an older brother to pass down his clothes to her like me. My shirts had air in them, not meant to be tucked in. She was primped, and her breasts or chest were plump like a chicken's. Her clothes fit on her body. She was eight. I saw the drawing of her hips, the shape of her armpits, and the route her arms took with her hands. She was brave.

"Patrick."

"Patrick?"

Like he wasn't good enough. Or cute enough. But he was a third grad-er. He was older so he was sexy. And he was there walking on the sidewalk to get to school, across the street from his cold dark house. I pointed and she looked.

Patrick.

Angie taught me about taste. What's a cute boy. I didn't know how to be picky. Her mother owned the Filipino market off Saviers and across the busy street was Fuwa, the only competition in the city. Her mother's face was round, her hair framed it with polished bangs and full wavy black hair. She had the perfect shade of lipstick, a pretty reddish maroon. She named her daughter Angeline, but to me, her mother was the white-faced angel.

Angie liked to gossip. Her face was dark like mine. With spots. I found out they were moles, but I wondered if she knew her face looked sick. Like a rat's, without whiskers. Her backpack was hanging behind her, classical pink. She taught me about kissing, boys, and bras.

The chain link fence was something to massage my fingers against when we walked along it to school. When I pointed at Patrick, I waved. I could feel my teeth open again as I talked about him. We were married.

The pompadour was natural on the top of his head. Like a crown. Taller than me. His dark skin against a plain white t-shirt and a pair of dark cotton shorts. His hands and his mouth are what I remember.

"Let's take a shower," he invited. And the place where a corner table would've been was where he put our shower. Pretend.

He took my hand I think. No one outside my family took my hand like that. I'm standing next to him. He pulls me to his body. Pretend keeps going. I was six. He was nine. I could feel breath and famine on him. And I went with it. His tongue became warm, moving inside my mouth. My teeth opened. His hair stood on top of his head, spilling into his sideburns. On the couch, I am lying underneath him. Sweat and salt from his lips heavy, questioning, curious. The curtains were always drawn. Such a dark house. So lonely. Like there was no electricity, except for the doorbell.

I had taken a shower with him in no water. I had slept on the couch with him and thought I should always sleep with someone's tongue moving in my mouth. Fingers turning my insides. My right side became cold after I left this cold house. He was the heat that kept me warm. My awkward body grew pink. Did I talk openly about him? Did my six-year old mouth not realize what a secret is?

"What did you do at Patrick's?"

"I took a shower," maybe I said.

"I slept in bed," maybe I said.

He didn't know me outside his cold, dark house. He wasn't in the story I was telling to Angie. He didn't know what I looked like if I wasn't taking a shower with him or sleeping next to him in his cold dark house. On the street, he couldn't tell the difference between me and some other little Filipino first grader. My heart sank as I waved at him. His face looked confused, looked past me, and he walked casually. Excited to go to school.

All You Ever Needed:
A Queer History of You

ADAM RABUY CRAYNE

In 2004 you go on your first date. You are 16 and he is 21. You have only been talking for two hours on DowneLink before he makes the impulsive decision to drive to your town. Hayward seems impossibly far from Union City, and you're happy he went through the trouble to reach you. His cologne is distinct and his teeth are perfectly straight. You pay for the movie tickets and he promises to pay you back eventually. When it's over, he drives you to the top of a hill, turns the heater up, starts playing Goapele on the radio, and brings you closer. It is nerve-racking and confusing, but this is the first time anyone has found you attractive, so you cooperate. You do it like the movies taught you and he exhales repeatedly. There is a foul taste in your mouth when it's over but you feel accomplished. He tells you that you aren't supposed to be as good as you are. It is the nicest thing anyone has ever said to you.

In 2005 he takes away the remnants of your innocence. You are 17 and he is 25. All it takes to convince you of his character is his Filipino blood and the fact you recognize him from previous yearbooks. The ride from school to his house and the walk from the front door to his bedroom are both silent. He only wants one thing from you, and that's fine. He goes in and out relentlessly, and when he's finished, you wonder why it never stopped hurting. Later that evening you ask your girlfriends if it was supposed to be that awful. The answers upset you: "Yeah, what did you expect?" "I wouldn't know. My first time wasn't up to me." "Well, he was

Filipino. That's probably why. Oh wait, you're Filipino, right? Sorry. I didn't mean it that way." The message is clear—Filipinos are dogs and you're one of them.

In 2006 he is different. All he wants is to hold your hand. He kisses you at Disneyland, takes you to his senior prom, and makes you believe in things like marriage and happily ever after. When he leaves for college you're convinced it's not worth worrying about because he loves you – he said it himself. Then one Thursday evening, he comes home for Spring Break and causes your heart to burst. He tells detailed stories about his experiences, reflects on how everyone is so intelligent and driven, and confesses how you simply don't measure up to what he needs in order to progress. Shattered, you spend the entire night drowning into your pillows, thankful your parents can't hear you gasping for air. And the next day, you go to school, fifteen minutes early for zero period as always, and saunter through the halls like a ghost half-withered away. You fail a history test. Calculus remains impossible. But you maintain your composure, only because it's offensive to be vulnerable around others. Your mother made it perfectly clear: Filipinos cry in the movies and in television shows, but never in public.

You rarely think of him in 2007 because college has you burgeoning with enthusiasm. San Diego is an intellectual refuge eight hours away from the mess you left behind, and plenty of groups appear willing to accept you. Some people think you are brown enough, and some think you are gay enough. But neither group allows you to be both. As you play tug-o-war with your identities, you find your confidence slowly diminishing. When you are passionate, they call you irrational. When you are calm they label you uncritical. They tell you repeatedly that you couldn't possibly understand Filipino American life, as if your mother's milk and blood do not flow within you. By day you read, write, present, march, and scream about Filipinos. At night you wonder if they will ever include you. In 2010 the university gives you a diploma to commemorate your work on a community that refuses to claim you. If he were around, he'd fight for you the way you fight for Filipino America, you're sure of it. But he isn't.

While the community sleeps among themselves you find solace in fucking strangers and relish in the fleeting moments you feel in control.

The ownership over your movement comes to an abrupt halt one October evening when he appears one day in your passenger seat, refusing to budge unless he is given a Round 2. It is wrong, but because you don't know anything but failure as a queer Pinoy, you give in. Only after dropping him off to his own car do you even consider calling the cops. On the way home, you find consolation in knowing the cops wouldn't have helped you in the first place.

In 2011 he turns your world upside down. You are a lost fresh graduate, oozing with an intense political agenda but bereft of a professional direction. He is a college dropout who cuts hair and has a tattoo above his buttocks. You two aren't supposed to work, and yet his jokes make you laugh. He listens to your stories and doesn't grow tired. He doesn't regard you as Filipino, but neither does the rest of the community. You try hard to ignore how desperately he wishes he could make his brown skin fade to white, and how he compares fucking other Filipinos to incest. It could be worse, you tell yourself.

He is amazing in bed. You learn that it's possible to feel just as good as he does. He calls you "babe" and "bitch" and you believe it's all out of love until he starts chiding you because you couldn't text back within the hour, because you didn't answer his question the way he deemed correct, because there are only so many hours in one day and you couldn't devote as many of your free ones to him. You recall arguments between your parents and family members and you assume this is merely an inevitable part of it all. But you also remember how, despite all the names he has given you, he never refers to you as his boyfriend. The moment the sting becomes too painful to ignore, he vanishes. Now you are the one lapsing into fits when your calls and texts go unanswered. Desperate for answers, you message him incessantly, lying and insisting it's okay if you just meet up for sex. Maybe if he sees you again, he'll snap out of it and regret ever having been so harsh. But even at your most shameless, he does not give into your propositions. You give up on him. You give up on love.

In 2012 you don't even know who he is – you just know he's inside you. You feel your eyes shifting from left to right more than you feel him thrusting into you from behind. As he ravages your body, your thoughts waver from contemplating what brought you here, an alley hidden behind rental cars that smells of urine, to wondering why none of your friends have come to your rescue. When it's over, you walk back to your car, force yourself to vomit, then drive home feeling disturbed, but lucid.

A cop pulls you over for going 70 and smells the vodka in your breath. If you even contest his accusations you will likely end up another person of color strewn on the side of the road filled with bullets, so you agree to spend the night in jail. Completely sober, a Black man to your right asks you what brought you here, and your thoughts begin to spiral. *Our people are disproportionately affected by alcohol usage and suffer from low self-image and intense internalized oppression. I don't even remember meeting him, saying hi, anything. I just remember his hands in between my legs, blinking, and waking up in the corner. When I drove home, I wasn't thinking about any of these things. I just wanted to sleep. Now I'm here.* You shrug your shoulders and tell him, "It's all bullshit." He laughs and gives you a high-five. Months later, you are given a free pass: the state has no case against you. Your HIV test comes out negative. You aren't overcome with joy like you thought you would be. You're simply relieved.

In 2013 you avoid him at all costs. Instead, you attend focus groups run by self-proclaimed experts about sexual health, Asian American social stigmas, and how to be kinder to yourself. In all these meetings, the leadership characterizes you as an angry and indignant soul without attempting to glean out the sources of your vitriol. You can't help but notice that their single coping mechanism is to go to the nearest bars and toss back their troubles. One meeting, you lose your patience and bluntly ask the group, "Damn, are we allowed to heal?" The silence that follows is a sufficient enough answer.

A job opportunity in the Philippines provides you with an escape route. You sign your life away for at least two years and trade your San Francisco cubicle for a classroom in Quezon City that feels like an inferno. You teach the children English and they teach you the limits of your blithe optimism. You learn that three years of Tagalog classes isn't enough. Linguistic prowess won't darken your skin. Your public school isn't and will never be their public school. You understand it all so much more clearly—you are not them and they are not you and their Philippines is not yours. Filipinos are not Filipino Americans and Filipino Americans aren't your

Filipino American, *so who the fuck are you then?* The confusion destroys you, but before you can give your employer the middle finger and begin packing your things, you meet him. The coincidences frighten you. He, too, has been chewed up and spit out and took the job to remind himself he has a purpose to fulfill. You bathe in each other's sweat and broken spirits, and every time he kisses you he sends the fractures of his heart into your own. You feel the pieces of yourself you assumed had dissolved to dust restoring inside you. In 2013 you are healing together.

In 2014 his healing stops. Those who broke him have long since deserted him, and since you are right beside him you receive his angst. He requests that you stop being so affectionate – it just reminds him of his demons. What about your own past, the demons you learned to ignore just for him? One afternoon you realize you're sapped of patience, so you call him and demand reciprocity. Several hours later you two are perched on a bench outside a church, eyes red and almost completely out of breath. With his last ounce of strength he bids you farewell. Home is several kilometers away but you still choose to walk. The next Monday, you lead a question and answer activity with your students. One child asks you who you love. A deluge of memories rushes through you – who ran away and who stayed – and you reply. "I love my students, I love my family, and I love my country. That's it." The next volunteer asks why you came to the Philippines. "I love my students, I love my family, and I love my country. That's it."

In 2015 you hit three strikes. You are in a motel room somewhere in Cubao with a tall and satisfactory lover whose name you never learned. He bends you and pounds you and ensures that you can't feel anything else but him. When he's finished, he reveals the extent of the lies he told you so you'd give in, and you bite your bottom lip to keep from screaming until your vocal cords give out. On the jeep ride home you pray to pass out. The next six months are the longest six months in your entire life. When September finally arrives you waste no time heading to the clinic. A haughty volunteer reads list after list of numbers about Filipinos and HIV infections before probing into your personal history. You are forced to revisit every instance in which you have been hurt, and when it's finally over, there is blood missing from your left arm, and your trauma is no longer yours alone.

As you return to the waiting room, your thoughts no longer revolve around him – they are entirely about you. Your head is ripe with questions about the weeks, months, and years ahead. How many do you have? How many do you deserve? You expect at any minute to break down but the tears never flow. Maybe, with all that has transpired, you have finally run out. The country and community have sapped you of your blood, your sweat, your tears, and with all your sacrifices, you're still left with an undeniable sense of hurt and loneliness. With all your shortcomings, perhaps your one option left to win the Philippines, Filipinos, and Filipino America over is to die for the country and for the people. As you make peace with your options, the volunteer returns with an envelope. You open it and exhale, taciturn. Non-reactive. Safe. Bailed out yet another time – you've lost count at this point. That night, you sit idly in bed wondering what makes you so special that despite the boundless ways you've failed as a Filipino American, you are permitted to keep dreaming. Are you worthy of the future you've been given?

You spend most of October deliberately reclusive. Then one Sunday morning, you are roused from your sleep by a strong heat. Your body feels lighter than usual, and as you walk toward the window, a gust of wind and the brightness of the sun hit you at once. In that instant it becomes clear: You have earned today and tomorrow. You are a survivor, and survival in a world committed to breaking you down is an act of heroism that ties you to your ancestors and your history more than anything. It is not yet your time to go, because the love you imagine for yourself and the people has yet to be realized. Until you find that transformative, sustainable, radical kind of love, it is worth it to keep fighting.

So when, in November, the boy you're dating begins verbally abusing you, you don't talk back or attempt to reason. You simply run fast. The further away you get, the wider you feel your lungs expanding. You have no clue where you are headed but there is security in knowing you're in charge, and that whatever happens next will be better. With every heartbeat, you feel a bitter memory lodged in your bones dissipating to make room for a new dream. This is the strongest you have ever felt.

In 2016 at last you find him, staring back at you in the mirror. His eyes are fiery with ambition and his smile carries promise for a Filipino America that is confident, certain, and worthy. He honors your struggle and massages the scars on your back so that they can sprout wings. He is prepared to lead with new ideas and build the community he knows is possible. You don't question why it took until now—what's important is that he's here now and will be there for you through every circumstance. He is beaming with wondrous love, and above all, he is in love with what he sees. He is all you ever needed.

CAUSE A STIR:
COALITIONAL
CONSCIOUSNESS
&
ORGANIZING

YSHMAEL CABANA

Cause a stir

The monsters have risen
lurking in between
Warm bodies of ocean
consuming the flesh of the poor.
This is the just flavour
of what is to come–
Rising levels of tension.
Lo, pressure's been raging
in this surge of emotions.
Will you concur?

We will lose
nothing along
but these chains
of a system falling down.

We'll sustain
in the gusts and the wind
by our mountains
in our own tongues, we speak
to build a new world
in dreams we've only seen
Decidedly we'll fulfill it, as we
cause a stir.

There the scar remains
in the aftermath
While counting the cost
is like carrying the weight of the world.

The measure of sacrifice
ought to be retold–
our monuments of suffering
and tests of strength and spirit
in the urge to be all resilient
Will you break?

We will lose
nothing along
but these chains
of a system falling down

We'll sustain
in the gusts and the wind
by our mountains
in our own tongues, we speak
to build a new world
in dreams we've only seen
Decidedly we'll fulfill it, as we
cause a stir.

Lani Paguio Felicitas

September 29, 2015

Dear Manong Emok, Manong Onel, and Manong Bello,

It brings tears to my eyes that your names have finally reached my lips. It took the murders of countless black men and women who have been slain by the same U.S. superpower that killed you, for me to realize that our struggles and our liberations are one and the same.

Manongs, I write this letter to you because our ancestors, comrades, and brothers and sisters in the Philippines, among the Pacific, and on Turtle Island do not understand what is at stake if we allow impunity and inaction. I want to learn your stories and the stories of our islands so I can agbiag! wake up! and share that knowledge with my brothers and sisters here on this land.

Manongs, allow me to explain how our oppressions and liberations are intertwined: similar to the Philippines paramilitary troops who occupy your learning centers, force evacuate your people, and make profit off your land through mining and monocrops, Corporate Corrections of America (CCA) are occupying Black, Hispanic, and Native American communities. CCA is force evacuating these children from schools to the prison system and generating revenue off of their bodies.

Since the beginning of U.S. colonization and imperialism, Black bodies and Filipino bodies have been under a system of discipline. What if our law enforcement and college professors taught us were taught to love and restore, rather than how to discipline and train? I inherited this "training" as I enter the university to gain the tools that create and perpetuate white supremacy and subordinate bodies that look like mine and yours and Black. This letter is the beginning to un-train myself, and restore the connections that I have lost with you.

111

I believe the strength of Lumad liberation is the strength of Black liberation and my liberation. So I ask that you allow me to hear your stories, and be patient as I learn these new languages that will set us free. I ask that you guide me to finding comradery on Turtle Island, among the Pacific Islands, and in the Philippines. In return, I will continue to defend the land and her people. I will continue to protect our water and share it with my brothers and sisters whom have no access. I will make sure that our children can inherit our wisdom so you can rest in peace and power.

I am ready to witness, to represent, to reimagine, and to restore.

With unfinished love,
Lani Paguio Felicitas

Lighting the Way

Keith Lara

What does it mean to be Filipino?
What is your vision for the future for the Filipino Community?

To the Filipino Community and its allies,

Being a Filipino is about being connected to our people on a level of compassion and understanding. We have our priorities in life and we hardly ever stray from them. Somewhere down the road, our priorities became skewed because of our desire for a "better life" meaning more wealth and a higher standard of living. However, wealth does not measure our worth as proud Filipinos. What makes our culture so special is that we celebrate our tradition with pride and understand that all we really have in this life are each other. Just to name a few examples, we put extreme emphasis on caring for our elders. We greet them with respect in any setting. A practice that Filipinos commonly do is reach for the hands of our elders and put their hand on our forehead as a sign of respect and as a way of asking for their blessing and guidance. This practice is called "manong" and it is a widely held tradition that will transcend generations regardless of how much change society undergoes. Also, another example of how we put emphasis on our countrymen, or as we like to call them, kapwa, is by always being hospitable. Growing up in the Philippines, I was privileged to witness my family and many other Filipinos illustrate hospitality with gracefulness and compassion. Whether it be a relative or a family acquaintance visiting the household, Filipinos never hesitate to offer food or say, "feel at home". We make everyone feel included and take initiative to be friendly and caring. Even when we didn't have a lot of food for our own family, we always tried to give to those who needed it more. Our hungers were often satisfied by the contentment of our neighbors. Food feeds the body but acts of kindness feed the soul. We understand this and often rely on our acts of charity for sustenance to get us through the day. I'd like to call us to action. I'd like to call for the revitalization of our communities as they were in the Philippines. I'd like our commonalities to intersect and rekindle the fire that burned in our ancestors' veins when they inhabited the Philippine Islands and masterfully carved a tradition that stands the test of time.

My vision for the future of the Filipino Community is that we all live life with some goal of improving our country. A lot of Filipinos immigrate from Home to the United States. A lot of them succeed in the U.S. attaining high paying jobs, and creating a stable life for themselves and their families. I'm so proud of our accomplishments here as immigrants because we are known as friendly and hardworking people. However, I challenge us to go well beyond that standard. I'd like us to return to our roots and remember where we came from. It's important to continue growing as a person and carve a path for ourselves but that path should involve giving back to the home country that has nurtured us for so long. My vision for a strong, united Filipino community is where we try to fight the injustices of our country and take control of our rights and freedoms. Acts of charity are important on a local level between fellow neighbors and acquaintances but I imagine a future where we gather together to create charities, programs, and any other such thing that could expand our compassion on a national level. Secondly and very importantly, a future I want us to secure for future generations should involve protests and political activism to combat the prevalent corruption that divides our beautiful country and diminishes our reputation on the world stage. All this can be done by those living in the homeland, those who have immigrated in search of a better life, and especially by those who are born abroad in foreign countries. The future I dream of for our beautiful country is one that is born out of the toil and sense of nationalism by Filipinos everywhere. Please, with all the talents that you have been born with, with all the wealth you may have amassed, please find a way to give back to our country. Understand that our life here on Earth is extremely limited. "I shall pass through this world but once. Any good, therefore, that I can do or any kindness I can show to any human being, let me do it now. Let me not defer or neglect it, for I shall not pass this way again" -Stephen Grellet. Fellow Filipinos, take pride in your roots, take pride in your accomplishments, take pride in each other, and be militant in your pursuit of our country's betterment.

Thinking about Philippine Studies in the United States in the 21st Century

Lily Ann B. Villaraza, Ph.D.;
Erina Alejo; Oliver Mangibin;
Klaine Justo; EdianBlair Schoefield

The Philippine Studies Department of the City College of San Francisco (CCSF) is 46 years young this year. When I joined the department in 2014, it should have been celebrating its 44th year. Instead, as the college began feeling the impact of the accreditation crisis through tumbling enrollment, increased class cancellations, diminishing class sizes, and the loss of many part-time faculty and staff, it was felt more deeply by smaller departments such as Philippine Studies. Our one full-time faculty member —our chair—retired as well, and the fight to have them appoint a new chair became a prolonged battle that lasted several months. I became the part-time chair after one year in the department. My predecessor held the position for less than a year, underscoring the volatile institutional condition that we continue to experience at CCSF. Since then, a question keeps appearing in various forms—in the reduction of our course offerings, in the lack of support to offer courses in sequence, in the suggestions that perhaps Philippine Studies would be better off folded into a larger department. The question? *What is the need and value of a Philippine Studies Department in American higher education? More specifically, what is its' role in a community college in the 21ˢᵗ century?*

This is a dangerous question to ask; the very posing of the question could be interpreted as uncertainty and lack of belief in the department's viability. Let me be clear: that is not the intention. But it would irrespon-sible of me to <u>not</u> address the question; without saying it out loud and addressing it directly, we cannot create the space to come up with solutions in the same way this department was birthed—together.

What I am suggesting is that the question be posed in a different way. For instance, *given the intimate political, social, economic, and cultural rela-tionship between the Philippines and the United States, why ISN'T there more attention given to the study of the Philippines in American higher education?* Or perhaps, *as Southeast Asia grows in visible importance to the global econ-omy, what do we understand about the nation-state that has been the U.S.' strongest ally in the Far East since the early 20ᵗʰ century?* Or perhaps even the following: *Acknowledging that Filipinos are the second largest Asian Pacific Islander American population in the United States, what do we know and understand about that immigrant and transnational conditions of this com-munity—and how can that understanding be utilized to serve this communi-ty better in social services, education, domestic policy, and civic engagement?* These are questions that the Philippine Studies Department—or any Area/Ethnic Studies department—could be addressing in their curriculum de-velopment, community engagement, and programming.

The Development of Philippine Studies[1]

It seems quite obvious, doesn't it—the answer to the question, "What is Philippine Studies?" Yes, of course, it means the study of the Philip-pines—the geography, the people, the culture and society of the archipela-go halfway across the world. Historically, was also a mechanism of colonial control through knowledge formation, disguised in the thing that many Filipinos desired after 300 years of Spanish rule: education.

Studying the Philippines was particularly important in the first half of the 20th century after the United States' claimed the archipelago as its'

---

[1] For a more detailed discussion on the historical development of Philippine Studies, please see Belinda Aquino's article "How Philippine Studies Began." Center for Philippine Studies. *How Philippine Studies Began.* University of Hawaii. http://www.hawaii.edu/cps/how-phil-ippine-studies-began/ [Accessed 4/20/16].

first and only official colony in 1898. American anthropologists, historians, economists, linguists, biologists, ethnologists, ventured out to the Philippines to measure heads, observe rituals, map languages, and establish schools to teach Filipinos how to be civilized and western. They formed opinions about the aptitude of Filipinos, unified the archipelago with a foreign tongue,[2] shaped the political landscape by supporting the studies of the Filipino elite in U.S. institutions, and placed them on display for the American public as a measured demonstration of the civilizing process.[3] By exercising control over the type of knowledge generated about the Philippines and its people, the United States shaped the way the world understood the archipelago and its inhabitants—even for the Filipinos themselves.

By the mid-20th century, the establishment of Philippine Studies departments and/or programs in colleges and universities was met with some enthusiasm as these power brokers in Philippine education returned home. Fueled by a desire to maintain an American presence in the Far East, institutions such as the University of Michigan and the University of Chicago worked to establish programs to forward the study of the Philippines. They also had vast troves of *Filipinana*—photographs, artifacts, and other knowledge bearing materials taken from the Philippines by academics building the Philippines' education system that demanded further study. But as major advocates for Philippine Studies like Fred Eggan and Joseph Ralston Hayden passed away,[4] Philippine Studies became a subset of Southeast Asian Studies. With the looming spectre of communism informing American foreign policy and US military involvement around the world by this time, as well as the eventual escalation of the Vietnam War by the late 1960's and early 1970's, studying the Philippines became less and less important.

---

[2] In developing a universal education system, the American colonial government made English the universal language and taught Filipinos in English.

[3] For more information, research "St. Louis World's Fair, 1904" or "Philippine Reservation, St. Louis.

[4] Joseph Ralston Hayden at the University of Michigan and Fred Eggan at the University of Chicago, to name two. The program at the University of Chicago was shut down in 1979, after Eggan's Death.

Philippine Studies at CCSF

This is not how the Philippine Studies Department at CCSF developed. Established in 1935, City College could not have hosted any of the *Pensionados*[5] that studied in the United States at the turn of the 20th century. CCSF, to our current knowledge, did not have faculty who had served in the American colonial government of the Philippines. As a community college, CCSF did not have ties to the Philippines in the way the University of Michigan or Berkeley did.

No, CCSF's Philippine Studies Department was birthed out of direct action and demand for more Filipino representation in the faculty and curriculum of the college by the Filipino community of San Francisco. At City College, the community and enrolled students banded together in the late 60's and early 70's—in the aftermath of the Third World Liberation Front's demands for the establishment of a College of Ethnic Studies at San Francisco State University—to lobby for the hiring of a Filipino counselor. They then worked toward the creation of an academic department to develop courses relevant to the Filipino community of San Francisco and the surrounding Bay Area. The Philippine Studies Department at CCSF was eventually established in 1970,[6] as the call for more relevant and reflective courses became a part of the call for representation, very much in the spirit of Ethnic Studies.

This is what makes the Philippine Studies Department at CCSF unique. From its conception, the department has straddled that line between Area Studies and Ethnic Studies. In straddling that line, questions of relevance, representation, and rigor surface; a) How do you make the study of a particular nation-state relevant to the broader understanding of our global community, b) Are these courses meant to speak specifically to Filipinos searching for their roots, and c) Is there an expectation that

---

[5] Pensionados were Filipino scholars (largely male) selected to study in the United States. The intention to prepare these men for leadership in politics and other sectors of civil society (education, economics, law, etc.) while exemplifying the benefits of assimilation to American patterns of behavior and thought.

[6] Archived newsclippings of the school newspaper, *The Guardsman*, revealed that Ruben Estandian, a student, and Jose Bonpua, Jr, a teacher at Serra High School, spearheaded the fight to establish the department in 1970.

these courses be easier for, or that the instructor be more lenient toward, the Filipino student? Some students have admitted that they enrolled in Philippine Studies courses thinking that they would 'easier' because they identified as Filipino—only to find that expectation was grossly overrated, but chose to stay because the material was fascinating. This, again, made me think about the value of these courses—their necessity in our institution.

Student Perspectives on the Importance of Philippine Studies

Four students—each various stages of their educational careers—were asked their take on the importance and value of Philippine Studies. I asked them about their understanding of the value of Philippine Studies in relation to their educational experiences and career trajectories. I also asked them who they thought would want to take these courses, and if they saw a need for Philippine Studies at all.

Their responses were at times surprising, at times expected, and all of it insightful. One student, who had already completed their bachelors, mentioned that this was the first time they were able to take "institutionalized Philippine Studies classes," something that students at their former university were still fighting for. Another student mentioned that they felt the department "…encourages students, including myself, to share personal anecdotes and narratives as a method of guidance and power to decolonized, transform, as well as change (and even assess) the dynamic in the Philippines and [among] Filipinos everywhere." That same student went on to say that they are "…thankful for this department because it creates, challenges, and provokes questions that are intended to foster growth…" Reflecting upon the connection between the Philippines, the United States, and the experience of Filipino immigrants in the U.S., one student commented that "…it challenges me to examine a country halfway across the world and analyze how the presence of Western powers altered its course of civilization while giving rise to ethnic nationalism…[and that] the merits that come with understanding [the Philippines] national and cultural transformation over time are essential to understanding immigrants in the U.S. and how this shapes our culture as Americans as well."

Other reactions spoke to the relevance of Philippine Studies to disrupting notions of privilege, of dominant culture, of equating power with whiteness, of the existence of a post-racial state, of difference. They felt the department provided space to think about colonial mentality, self-worth and the perpetuation of self-hate; about culture, cultural norms, and the role culture plays in identity development. For the Filipino students, it provided opportunity for self-reflection and making connections, to think about the differences and similarities between Filipinos and Filipino Americans—and how that is no longer bound by borders or language proficiency. For non-Filipino students, Philippine Studies courses provide opportunities to draw connections to other communities' experiences and struggles.

One student spoke to the department's relevance to a pluralist educational experience; that it provides students with the opportunity to compare, contrast, and critically analyze the macro and micro relationships between States and Nations, and how they impact interactions among individuals. They pointed out that the institution has placed greater value on "financially promising departments [that emphasize] STEM, without giving thought to the fact that "…this disproportionate discourse will continue to deter students from accessing vital information about the narratives and identities [of] people who have helped shape the internal and external dynamics of this country…" In other words, students do not to take Philippine Studies courses because it is not within the scope of their career trajectory. These blinders also do not encourage dialogue and understanding, nor a well-rounded knowledge base that help our youth understand their importance to the communit(ies) they exist in.

R/Evolution

There are two primary goals for many students who attend community college; a) complete general education courses then transfer to a 4-year institution as quickly as possible, or b) to earn a certificate to enter the workforce. As such, there is little room and time to explore courses that encourage understanding of the socio-cultural bonds that define our daily lived experiences. Community college students may take one or two courses in the humanities or social sciences to fulfill a requirement. If an interest is sparked but then not supported (institutionally, by family, by peers), or a career path is to not clearly tied to a course, why continue pursuing that course of study? If a class is not within the scope of a student's educational plan, or if it does not fulfill certain requirements, students are not encouraged to take them. Even worse, if a student is on a scholarship and a course they are interested in taking does not 'fit' in the scope of that scholarship, they are faced with the decision of either a) paying for the course out of pocket, or b) dropping the course because they cannot afford it. Institutionally, this impacts the departments that offer arts, humanities, social science, and intersectional courses that provide students the opportunity to engage learning in a way that is significant to them. These sorts of restrictions could have serious implications in our ability to send forth our graduates with a well-rounded education.

So back to the original question: *What is the need and value of a Philippine Studies Department in American higher education? More specifically, what is its' role in a community college in the 21ˢᵗ century?* Colleagues who attended CCSF as students in the 80's and 90's shared that it was through Philippine Studies that they were able to find themselves, to learn about their culture and community. I empathize with that sentiment; it was through studying Filipino language and Philippine/Filipino American history that I was able to firmly ground my sense of self. As we move through the 21ˢᵗ century, and as youth have far more access to wonderful community-based entities (i.e. Galing Bata) and programs in other institutions (i.e. the Pinoy/Pinay Educational Partnership) providing spaces to explore their identities long before they reach college, it is clear that the trajectory of Philippine Studies, as it exists particularly at the community college level, needs to evolve.

This essay was not meant to provide answers. It is an exercise—and perhaps an indulgent one—to muse about the past, present, and future of Philippine Studies as we struggle to redefine its relevancy in the institutional context of a community college. But as the US is poised to reopen military installations in the archipelago, as the Philippines struggles with an accelerated "brain drain" phenomenon, as the Bay Area is home to the largest Filipino population—immigrant and American born—in the

United States, and as the global community becomes smaller and more connected, I have confidence that the Philippine Studies Department at CCSF will remain relevant.

JANICE LOBO SAPIGAO

What stands the test of time?

My mom is going to the Philippines next month, and I am afraid for her. For the first time in fifteen years, since my grandma passed away, she is going this time for more personal matters, ones that call her and only her home. My brother and I spent the day with my mom buying pasalubong, to give to our fam who don't have much there. Lotions, t-shirts, candy, lipsticks. I read a headline the other day that said that any immigrants may be barred from reentering the US because of Trump's illegal ban. The thought of that reality kept me in bed all day, three days this week. Today, airports are sites of protest, everywhere is a necessary site of protest. In 2006, I wrote in an essay somewhere that I thought airports were the saddest and scariest places in the world. She is leaving Trump's fascist America to travel to her first home, now Duterte's corrupt and dictatorial Philippines. She first left during Marcos's reign in the middle of martial law, and now what is the difference. 1978 and 2017. My mom won't be traveling back or to any time. They are the same.

Kirin Amiling Macapugay

Paradise Hills, 1994.

Because when some dude is walking towards you and your friends
with a gun in his hand, cocked sideways, you run.

You run before you can even make sense of what's happening, or gather
your bearings, or fear he might have just followed you.

Your heart is beating as you crouch behind your dad's old van, hoping
they can't hear you breathe, hoping your friends are okay.

You think about how just a few years ago you watched them lower
another friend into the ground. How the jacket they dressed him in
covered the big hole in his chest, left there by a bullet at close range.

But that's another story.

A story they had in the papers, and how the journalists stressed he was his
parents' only child, an added jolt of tragedy.

And you think for a brief second, "am I next?"

And then suddenly it's quiet.

And then you hear the crying.

You remember the relief of seeing your friends alive, and the horror that
one is bleeding, and he's bleeding into your auntie's carpet in the living
room your friends dragged him to.

But he's alive.

You're all alive.

The news crews and the police arrive, the spinning lights from the top of the cop cars blend in with the red lights on the cameras.

It's all lights and sirens and voices, and you wonder if the cameras caught you crying.

They did.

Then his mom and sisters get to your house, you watch them weeping and wailing on the couch, holding each other and rocking and screaming "why?"

You do your best to tell them it'll be okay.

You hear your words float out of your mouth, but you don't really know what they mean.

Because you can't understand how this happens to you and your neighborhood, to your community.

So many, many times.

HOW TO MAKE HOME:
FAMILY
&
RADICAL PARENTING

Learning to Breathe: Pinayist Dialogues between Mother and Daughter

Heartbeat @ 3 years old

Mahalaya: Mama, Why are you crying?

Mom: I'm just really stressed out.

Mahalaya: Why?

I remember watching my mom put together the binders for her tenure at the dinner table. Letter after letter, from student after student, it seemed endless. I wondered why she was so sad.

Mom: I don't know if I can explain why.

All the while, I am thinking that this child at three wouldn't be able to understand my fears and guilt of not being able to raise her—how a mother is naturally suppose to know how to do. I'm suppose to give up everything for her, right? I'm suppose to console her when she's upset. How could this three-year-old baby even understand what I'm going through as a community engaged-Pinay-professor, pretending to be a mother. Pressures of being a good Pinay. Pressures of being a good professor. Pressures of being a good mother. I didn't feel I was really real in any of those identities. No longer did my impostor's syndrome only affect my identity as a scholar but it seeped into all my insecurities of not being a good mother. My tears came from the severity of my anxiety that I may not receive the tenure necessary to keep my job, which also meant, I would not be able to provide for my child.

MAHALAYA: Come here mama.

I put my hands on my mom's face and watched the tears drip from her eyes down her cheek and onto my hands. I slowly put her head to my chest positioned to hear me breathe.

MOM: I'm just so scared. I'm afraid I can't take care of you.

I wept as I listened to her heartbeat, remembering that this child, who had slightly premature birth, suffered from a premature heart which caused a number of hospitalizations and an endless series of sleepless nights caring for her, worrying if she would ever mature. And there she was breathing.

MAHALAYA: It's okay mama, I'll take care of you because you always take care of me and so many other people too. Can you hear my heartbeat?

MOM: Yes, lovebug, it's like music.

So much clarity in that moment. She taught me how to see my purpose. A doctor, but not that kind of doctor; sure enough a doctor that listens to people's breathing, their heartbeats, their stories. My vocation is to listen deeply to their narratives to see what they need and provide what is necessary for them to continue to breathe. This I learned from listening to my own child's heartbeat.

Heartbreaking and Heartmending @ 5 years old

MAHALAYA: She said I was too dark. Why did she say that? Am I too dark?

MOM: She's wrong. You are beautiful.

I was completely heartbroken, hearing my child say that another child told her she was too dark. I thought, why does happen? Why so early? Not sure if she was even prepared to handle it.

MAHALAYA: That's oppression, right?

I learned that word in my PEP (Pin@y Educational Partnerships) afterschool class and I was so proud that I knew how to use it. My mom started PEP to teach teachers how to teach Ethnic Studies focused on Pinays and Pinoys to kids like me all the way from kindergarten to college. I really don't know a life without Ethnic Studies. I was pretty much born into PEP.

MOM: Yes, it's racism. It's based on a system of white supremacy, where people think and act on the belief that white is better than any other color.

Okay, I was not sure if it was going to make sense to a five year old kinder-gartner. I mean, can we teach about racism to kids?

MAHALAYA: Hm, that's like the three I's of oppression, right? I learned in PEP that INSTITUTIONAL oppression is like the laws that make it okay to be racist, then the INTERPERSONAL is like what that girl said to me, and the INTERNALIZED is like if I let it get to me and I end up hating myself because I'm a brown Pinay.

I remember feeling so clever that I was able to use what I learned in my PEP class. I also felt I was channeling my inner Ninang Dawn (Mabalon).

MOM: Yes, thank you for PEP!

Shocked and thrilled at the same time, I was so thankful that my child was being educated by amazing teachers in her PEP afterschool pro-gram. In many ways, PEP was my first baby...teaching the baby that I birthed how to live in this world that is oftentimes cruel and filled with all kinds of oppressions. But Mahalaya had PEP to ground herself, to teach her how to breathe in this socially toxic world.

MAHALAYA: (a couple of years later) : Can I have monster cupcakes with three eyes this year? And I'll make sure to give cupcakes to all of those who might have self-hatred so that I can teach them to take a bite out of oppression.

And they were purple ube cupcakes.

Dancing with Heart @ 7 years old

MOM: What do you dance with?

MAHALAYA: My heart.

MOM: Then why are you so sad?

Mahalaya danced since she was three years old and she always trusted her heart. Since her very first performance, I knew she had something special. Our ritual backstage always went beyond makeup, costumes, and warming up. It always includes a centering moment. A whisper in her ear, I would alway ask, "What do you dance with?" and without a doubt, she always said, "My heart." But there was one time when her confidence was shot.

MAHALAYA: I'm never going to be good enough.

I saw all the girls at the competition, most them were taller than me, with good feet, turn-out, and flexible legs that kicked past their heads. And there I was, pigeon-toed-sickled feet with knobby knees, the kid who was the last one in class to be able to do the splits and pretty much smaller than everyone else. There was a time when I thought I really didn't have a chance because all I had was heart.

MOM: Why do you compare yourself to others?

MAHALAYA: I don't know. I'm just not as a good as other girls.

Not too many people know this but there was a time when one of the girls that I danced with told me I was the worse one in class. She even pushed me to go to the back of line when we were going to do our across-the-floor combinations. I wanted to believe that she was just being mean, but it really stuck with me. This was combined with being told that did not having the natural skills needed to be a classical ballerina. This may all come as a surprise to people who only see the selected photos that my mom chooses to post on Facebook.

MOM: You are amazing and you dance with your heart.

I wasn't sure how to get her to believe in herself. I could see the tears running down her face and I was heartbroken.

MAHALAYA: But I'm not the best one. I mean, I won't win anyways.

MOM: But you move with your heart...

MAHALAYA: But it's not enough...

MOM: Enough for what?

MAHALAYA: I just don't know if I'm special.

MOM: Do you realize that your dancing has so much power? When the music starts, I can feel you breathe. From the moment that your body begins to move, I can see that you are beyond grace, it's pure joy. You tell stories and counterstories with your movement. You carry the legacy of your babaylan ancestors in your spirit. You mend soul wounds that have withstood many generations of trauma. You are a vessel of critical hope. Your dancing is medicine. Your dancing is healing.

MAHALAYA: Like when you listen to my heartbeat?

MOM: Dancing is breathing. Each movement is a breath. So, what do you dance with?

Anytime before she gets on stage, I ask her this question. Her answer is as practiced as the dance itself.

MAHALAYA: My heart.

I never had a problem dancing with my heart. Without dancing with your heart, you're just doing blank moves. Even my commitment to improving my technique in dance, I do with my heart. My mom taught me from the very beginning that dancing isn't worth doing if I don't do it from the heart. Actually, she pretty much taught me to do everything with my heart.

Beating Hearts @ 12 years old

MOM: Why are you so calm?

This child organically lives out the meaning of her name, Mahal=Love and Malaya=Freedom.

MAHALAYA: I'm a pisces, I'm water. When the water is peaceful it's all nice and flowy, but when I get stressed out, there is a tsunami. There's no in between.

I'm not the only pisces in my family. I come from a matriarchy of fish beginning with my Lolas who are some of the strongest women that I know. They've swam oceans to ensure our family's survival. We, fish swim in schools. Schools that teach Kapwa, I am you and you are me. We, fish swim in schools that are cohesive and calm until we are being hunted or attacked.

MOM: What do you stress out about? Do you ever worry about fitting in?

I often ask Mahalaya questions about her social life. Every night we have conversations about our day where we share moments of fear and efforts of bravery.

MAHALAYA: What is the reason to fit in? We were all born to stand out, right? I mean we all have people who we admire and aspire to be like. Like in dance, there's people that I look up to and hope I can be as good as them one day but I don't want to be them, because I am me.

MOM: Then, what do you stress out about?

MAHALAYA: Big things, like, people are getting hunted and tortured.

MOM: What do you mean? Nightmares?

MAHALAYA: No, like real things that are happening in our world. Like inside my heart, I worry about my daddy. I worry about him walking on the street. Because people who look like him are getting killed everyday. I even worry about my cousins who are Black because we live in a nation that doesn't respect that #blacklivesmatter.

I remember watching a Black man get killed on Instagram by a police officer. I watched his girlfriend watch. I watched his daughter watch. This is the night that I won the National Junior Outstanding Dancer Award from NYCDA (New York Dance Alliance). My mom thought I couldn't sleep because of excitement of winning but really I couldn't sleep because I couldn't stop thinking about a the Black man that was killed. I couldn't sleep because of Kapwa.

MOM: Do you remember the man who was killed by a police who strangled him? He kept saying, "I can't breathe."

MAHALAYA: Yes, I remember you giving a presentation on it during a workshop for teachers at the Free Minds, Free People conference.

At this same conference, I did a dance called, "I See Fire" and the focus was on solidarity with the #blacklivesmatter movement.

Mom: I can't sleep sometimes thinking about all the people whose right to breathe has been taken from them.

Mahalaya: You and I are a lot alike then. I believe our purpose is to help people breathe again. You teach teachers how to breathe so they can teach their students to breathe.

Mom: And when you dance, your breath in each movement gives the world a chance to breathe again, to live again. But, we're both going to have to learn to sleep, to rest so that we can continue to pursue our purpose.

Mahalaya: It's been a while mom, since you've listened to me breathe.

Mom: I think it's time again. I miss the music of your heartbeat.

RAISING REVOLUTION:
CRITICAL PIN@Y PARENTING

RODERICK DAUS-MAGBUAL, ED.D
ARLENE DAUS-MAGBUAL, ED.D

Growing up in America, the search for identity is a common journey for many children of Filipino immigrant families. For the both of us, growing up as second generation Filipina/o Americans, understanding who we are between the worlds of school and home was a balancing act. The pressures of assimilation at school required us to sacrifice our culture in terms of language; attempting to fit in where majority of our classmates and teachers were white; and squeezing our identities into an American educational system that was relegated to a couple of paragraphs. Our praxis of parenting stemmed from this oppression where our purpose to become Ethnic Studies educators was motivated to create a sense of community for youth of color, to legitimize the narratives of our students, and how we utilize their understanding of themselves to create a sense of purpose and a commitment to transforming their communities. From our experiences in organizing with students, communities, and now our family, these factors have been influential in shaping our parenting that encompasses social justice, love and hope. In this essay, we will specifically focus on two pillars and how it informs our practices of parenting towards raising revolution. The two pillars we will discuss are: (1) Pinayism and how this philosophy and orientation challenges gender roles and expectations of fatherhood as it pertains to Pinoys and (2) Freire's (1970) "reading the world" and how these foundational concepts have configured Critical Pin@y Parenting (CPP).

Fathering & Pinayism

As a Pinoy in America, we are influenced by many factors to what it means to be a "man." In my Ilokano American family, my father, Amante Magbual, and a few of my uncles held the primary roles as cook, handyman, and as the stay-at-home parent, while my mom and aunties worked either the graveyard or day shifts as nurses. Although, I witnessed my dad prepare my mother's meals for work, iron her uniform, and balance the family checkbook, Filipino "machismo" was overwhelmingly present in what it means to be a "man." The social and cultural expectations and pressures through popular culture, the absence of younger critical Pinoy role models, and the rites-of-passage among friends and family were core influences that molded my world perspective and actions. My experiences through high school, college, graduate school, and working in various youth and community based organizations allowed me to reflect and redefine what it means to be a radical Pinoy father. One of the main concepts that allowed me to be vulnerable, reflective, and be in solidarity with my Pinay sisters is the praxis of Pinayism. In this section, we will discuss what Pinayism is and how it constructed my understanding of fatherhood in our philosophy and practice of parenting.

According to Tintiangco-Cubales (1996) Pinayism is described as centering the discourse on the lives, experiences, and issues of Pinays in the global, local, and personal contexts. It is a revolutionary action that involves pain + love = growth in addressing the inequities that Pinays face (Tintiangco-Cubales, 1996). One of the misconceptions about feminism or womanism, is that it is "man-hating" or exclusive to only women, but Pinayism calls for Pinoys to be engaged in the process of dialogue and action. Tintiangco-Cubales (2005) articulated:

> Pinoys must learn to engage in the conversation on Pinayism so that they may better understand a more complete rendition of the struggle of "Filipinos in America." Pinayism does not just serve the needs of Pinays it also serves the Pinay/Pinoy community as a whole (p. 142).

Samson (2005) further expressed, "The responsibilities of Filipino American feminist men must then move from challenging individual thoughts

\and the development of a Pinayist consciousness to Pinayism as a way of life, a way of being in the world" (p. 160). Fatherhood interpreted through a Pinayist lens allowed me to uncover the blind spots of privilege as a heterosexual Filipino American man in creating an equitable space with my asawa while redefining what it means to be a Critical Pin@y parent.

Fathering through a Pinayist praxis allowed me to contextualize, appreciate, and embody the work of Pinays in my life in nurturing my sense of self. What I learned from my grandmother, mother, wife, and especially Pinay mentors, is to learn how to listen, reflect, and have the courage to take on the roles that have been relegated to Pinays where Pinoys have benefitted because of heteropatriarchy. Samson (2005) encourages:

> Filipino American men committed to Filipina American feminist struggle must also begin to challenge and transform the patriarchal family. The patriarchal family is built around the sexist and gendered division of labor that includes domestic work as well as parenting responsibilities. The sexist and gendered division of housework must be abolished, and men must take more responsibility in sharing the day-to-day tasks of maintaining a residence and household. There must also be a reevaluation of the parenting responsibilities (p. 162).

Dedicating my life to social justice requires one to acknowledge their privilege and systems that are in place that sustains them. It also calls for Pinoys to take action by developing a space of equity with their partners. Samson (2005) further expressed for Pinoys to, "Experiment… with new forms of family life are ways of prefiguring possible social and household relationships" (p. 162). In practical approaches to addressing gender roles and expectations as a father, I play a critical role with my wife as our children's first teachers. I learned to reflect on what the traditional roles that the women in my family have undertaken and how I take on those roles in serving the family inside and outside the home. This meant in addition to my professional career, I engaged in assisting my wife in becoming the family's cook, doing the laundry, bathing the children, helping our daughter with her homework, learning how to do a ballet bun, putting on makeup for our daughter's recital practices, driving my daughter and her friends to dance classes, and dancing our infant son in the middle of night. This is the least I can do for my wife who sacrificed her mind, body and soul by bringing life into this world.

Reading the World and Parenting

Parenting has become our new process of decolonization where we have learned and engaged in cultivating critical spaces for our family and community. Freire (1970) expressed, "I am not in the world simply to adapt to it, but rather to transform it" (p. 7). The redefinition of our roles as community engaged parents was needed to deconstruct social norms and also to expand the possibilities of what it means to be Filipina/o in America. This is more than a personal endeavor, it is rooted in a community need and the urgency to transform parenting towards incorporating social justice, equity, and decolonization. "Reading the world" is having the historical, social, political, and cultural literacy to "read" the text of oppression in our our world and the engagement that is required to address central problems in our communities (Tintiangco-Cubales, 2010; Friere, 1970). In this section we will discuss how Freire's (1970) concept of "reading the world" and its relationship to parenting.

Parents become part of their children's communities physically, emotionally, and politically. Freire (1970) described, "The world—becomes the object of that transforming action by men and women which results in their humanization" (p.86). The reciprocal relationship of learning and parenting informs parents' purpose to address the inequities and injustices of the larger community. This revolutionary act embodies the hope and courage to transform the world through humanization of self and others. We found that community building and action as parents build a strong foundation of critical relationships between mothers, fathers, children, and our communities.

Central to reading the world is understanding the various systems of oppression that operates on a daily basis. Issues such as race, class, gender, and sexuality are just a few forms of domination that must be incorporated in parenting. Matias' (2016) Critical Race Parenting (CRP) discusses the importance of understanding dominant discourses of race by teaching and learning with your children the larger dynamics and complexity of racism that influence our lives. CRP becomes an educational praxis that can engage both parent and child in a mutual process of teaching and learning that centralizes race (Matias, 2016). In reading the world, we must have the courage to discuss issues that is considered taboo in our culture to the forefront, in order to deconstruct and reconstruct spaces of power. To discuss race with children at a young age provides them with a critical consciousness at a young age to become the change they want to be in the world. This is crucial in nurturing our children to become a future filled with love, hope, and possibility.

Raising Revolution

The concepts of Pinayism, "reading the world" and Ethnic Studies have been instrumental in shaping our parenting. Communities that will love, raise, and teach our children and give them the hope that is integral to CPP. Parenting is not exclusive to the household, but also takes into consideration the communities where they reside. As we think about the ways in which we raise our children, we think about how our children will be raised within the context of education. Will our children have a community of educators, artists, and leaders that will guide their understanding of self? How can they reach their potential and be active participants in society? Or, will they have to submit to traditional forms of education that masks their issues under color blind racism and the myth of meritocracy? Will our children receive the attention and services they need to succeed in school and in life? Raising revolution through CPP is challenging, but thinking about the community that will help raise our children throughout their lives is essential in developing a transformative identity that leads to action. In this section, we will discuss our process in raising our children in discussing issues of race and racism and our role as parents.

Oscar Grant, Trayvon Martin, Mike Brown, Tamir Rice, Eric Garner, Sandra Bland, Freddie Gray, Alton Sterling, and Philando Castille, are just a few names that have captured headline news, as our nation grapples with the complexities of race, racism, police brutality and understanding of #blacklivesmatter. Shows such as ABC's *Blackish* have brought stories to American households talking about parenting, raising Black children, and the Black Lives Matter movement. One of the main storylines from

Blackish and common Facebook stories, which focus on the "talk" about raising Black children and encounters with police, we reflected on our early experiences as children learning about policing and authority from our Filipina/o immigrant parents. We wondered, "Did we have these 'talks' with our parents?" "Do white kids have these 'talks?'" We both shared a common experience about our parents telling us to comply with the police, never to eyeball them, and "not rock the boat." As young adults we found that the police have manipulated and harassed us for being identified as gang members, pulled over for "fitting the profile," and padded down for "our safety." We would get into arguments with our parents about how authority would treat us like criminals for doing nothing and our parents would blame us for doing something when we never did. We wondered, where did this sense of compliance and accommodation stem from? As Ethnic Studies educators, we found it important for our children to connect the history of violence that our parents have experienced because of the legacies of Spanish and American colonialism in the Philippines and the result of state violence upon its own people. It is important for our kids to understand the connection and solidarity between Black Lives Matter and our experiences as Filipina/o Americans.

Amianan, our eldest child, sat besides us while watching the protests unfold in Ferguson, Missouri after the slaying of Mike Brown and she asked, "What is Black Lives Matter?" "Why are the police doing this to people?" We could have dismissed the situation and gave her a generic response such as, "You'll understand when you get older." Raising revolution embodies the courage and hope to transform the world through humanization of self and others (Freire, 1970; Daus-Magbual & Tintiangco-Cubales, 2016). It takes courage to engage your children in dialogue and to have the faith in them to understand right and wrong. We began a discussion with Amianan by asking: Is this right? Is it okay for the police to draw their weapons on an unarmed person with their arms in the air? Was it right for the cop to take a person's life? Amianan silently and reflectively replied, "No, it's not right." These moments become learning opportunities to wrestle with challenging questions that parents can easily dismiss, but are life changing experiences for children.

We find it important for our children to understand race, racism, and its relationship to state violence upon marginalized people in our society and creating solidarity movements in addressing these issues. Raising our children comes with a world of contradictions or dialectical relationships of ideology. How do we give the freedom to our children to make mistakes and learn from them but also guide them with authority so they can make conscious decisions for themselves? What does it take to lead our children to understand their context and transform it from the oppression that exists in our community, society and the world? We want our children to have a community where people are transforming their own lives and supporting those around them.

Conclusion

Our daughter Amianan and son Razón are symbols in this essay of Filipina/o American children being raised in a conscious and politically engaged community. With the hopes and dreams that Amianan and Razón will live their lives that examines their history, identities and become active participants in naming and transforming the world they have inherited. In trying to understand our experiences as young Filipina/o Americans, we have to gain a deeper understanding of the oppression that many Filipina/o Americans face in the United States and why our experiences often go unnoticed.

WORKS CITED

Daus-Magbual, A., Tintiangco-Cubales, A. (in press) Ethnic studies and the development of a critical leadership praxis. *White Washing American Education: The New Culture Wars in Ethnic Studies* (Praeger Publishers, Fall 2015)

Freire, Paulo. 2000. *Pedagogy of the Oppressed*, 3rd edition. New York: Continuum International.

Freire, Paulo. 2000. *Pedagogy of the Oppressed*, 3rd edition. New York: Continuum International.

Matias, C. E. (2016). "Mommy, is being Brown bad?": Critical Race Parenting in a "Post-Race" Era. *Journal of Race and Pedagogy*. 1(3). Article 1. http://sound ideas.pugetsound.edu/rpj/vol1/iss3/1

Samson, F. (2005). Filipino American men: Comrades in the Filipina/o American feminism movement. In M.L. De Jesús (Ed.), Pinay power: Peminist critical theory (p. 149-166) . New York: Routledge Taylor & Francis Group.

Tintiangco-Cubales, A. (2005). Pinayism. In M.L. De Jesús (Ed.), *Pinay power: Peminist critical theory* (p. 137-148). New York: Routledge Taylor & Francis Group.

Decolonizing Pinay Motherhood

Maria J. Ferrera
Cecily Relucio Hensler

How do we, as Pinay motherscholars, raise our biracial daughters to love themselves and the ways of being of their ancestors and anitos? What possibilities does mothering hold for healing our families' immigration traumas and generations of Pilipinx colonial wounding?

We share this story as a dialogue, in order to preserve the uniqueness of our voices and experiences and to illustrate the importance of *pakikiisa* —making space for unity and mutual support—within the isolating culture of whiteness that permeates our daily lives. In recognizing our interdependence and the sacredness of our bond as Pinays, we liberate ourselves from individualism and competition, and restore our precolonial values of collectivism and *kapwa*.

Honoring Our Trauma

CECILY: We met a few years ago at a conference; I went to your presentation on 2nd-generation Filipinx-Americans' mental health. I've battled depression for much of my life, but until I heard your research, I had no idea that my struggles had anything to do with being 2nd gen Fil-Am. But what I was most drawn to was your life story and how much we have in common—being Pinay, married to white partners, raising daughters, working in academia. Growing up in the Midwest and assimilating into mainstream white culture. And you were kind enough to remember me and invite me to DIWA.

MARIA: Yes! We had an immediate connection when you introduced your self. It's been rewarding to work with you, facilitating dialogue and community outreach through DIWA, which is about whole health—mind, body and soul—in and of our Fil-Am community.

CECILY: I really needed DIWA. Becoming a mother was traumatic for me on so many levels! In the first year I knew that things weren't right. But it wasn't until a few years later--when I was in crisis and my personal life was unravelling—that I found a therapist who enabled me to do the work I needed to do to be healthy. It's helped me to understand mental illness in my family: how my dad's mental illness dominated our family dynamic, how it impacted my mother and my relationship to her. My mom died when I was 24, and we had a complicated relationship and a lot of unresolved issues. All of those things were impeding my day-to-day functioning, especially as a mother and a partner.

MARIA: You mentioned that you see connections between your father's mental illness and his upbringing in the Philippines.

CECILY: Linda Pierce, a Pinay mestiza scholar, writes, "The skeletons in my closet did not belong to me alone."[1] She insists that Pinxys situate our personal and familial histories within the histories of our collective experiences as a people. I wanted to understand how that applied to my family and me, so I started looking into our family history, asking a lot of questions of family members. I learned about Tondo, where our family is from. It's an extremely poor, notoriously "rough" area of Manila. This discovery helped me to recognize our familial culture of interpersonal violence as a result of intergenerational poverty. Putting these pieces together led me to the realization that it was more than just my father. The things our family was carrying were much larger than us--they're rooted in socioeconomic injustice, which is a legacy of centuries of colonization of the Philippines.

---

[1] Pierce, L. M. (2005). Not just my closet: Exposing familial, cultural, and imperial skeletons. In M. L. De Jesus (Ed.), *Pinay power: Theorizing the Filipina/American experience* (pp. 31-44). New York: Routledge.

MARIA: As you're talking, I'm remembering a moment from the Center for Babaylan Studies Conference. A woman said, *"We're all scarred."* We're scarred collectively, but also individually, you know, in different ways. Like you, I'm trying to make connections with my own heritage and history. My profile is typical in many ways: two professional parents, one an engineer, one a nurse, settling into a predominantly white suburb. I was incredibly introverted, and I'm not sure if that's my personality, or if that's a result of being Filipina, being different, being darker skinned. No one ever told me that you're on the outside looking in. But that's certainly how I felt. My parents were truly loving parents, but I don't think they—we—had the words for my experience growing up. It was a struggle growing up feeling invisible. As an adult, learning about colonial mentality and internalized inferiority, I can see that I carry that. Feeling like I'm on the outside. Always investing energy in trying to prove myself. Sometimes there are no words to describe that experience. What is my trauma? Is it legitimate to name it that way? Because in many ways I've been privileged as well. How do we articulate it to other people who don't understand what it's like? There's a fear of being dismissed, of being seen as overdramatic. But there is legitimacy in how we internalize messages from our parents about who we are, based on how they've internalized who they are in the world.

CECILY: That goes back to the idea of being scarred. The wounds eventually heal, but the scar tissue is there as a reminder. The idea isn't to get back to a place where your skin is flawless as though…

MARIA: …the wounds never happened.

CECILY: Right. How can we see our scars as a mark of our strength, resilience, and ability to heal ourselves? There's an indigenous concept, *blood memory*. We carry the trauma of the dehumanization of our people and the dispossession of our land and resources—our birthright—even if we don't realize it. Our inner voices tell us *something's not right*. But we internalize that feeling as being about us instead of the society in which we live—its racist violence and colonial logics. That's why decolonizing is so important, so we can learn the things that have been obscured from our view in order to keep us from being free, from being whole.

MARIA: What's been helpful is the idea that I'm always evolving. I'm more aware and conscious and healthier in terms of dealing with things differently, accepting that our trauma doesn't disappear. It's an especially tender place all the time. I don't know why I'm starting to tear up!

CECILY: It's okay. It's part of the process. I thought about that earlier, like should I get some tissues ready? One or both of us might cry. [*shared laughter*]. I believe that the individualistic culture of this society cuts us off from each other. We suffer in isolation, not realizing how much we need that connection with others whose experiences resonate with our own.

Building an Altar[native] with our Daughters

MARIA: Let's talk about how our processes of trauma and healing manifest themselves in our mothering. What do our daughters teach us about what it means to be Pinay?

CECILY: I took Vanessa and Mia to an event at the Field Museum, *Pamanang Pinoy*, which I think means Pilipino heritage. The museum "owns" 10,000 Pilipino artifacts, appropriated in the early 1900s when the U.S. began its occupation of our motherland. The aim of the event was to acknowledge the journeys of these—our—sacred objects and to heal and liberate them from the imperialistic intentions of the white Americans that brought them here. Each object had an altar made from a banana leaf, a bowl of water, a candle, rice and pesos. After the ceremony I asked to take some rice and a banana leaf. Mia is tactile and enjoyed running her fingers through the rice, and that was the extent of my thinking. But when we got home, she asked, "Can I make an altar to Lola? Because this is the way that Filipinos do it. I want to do it in that way." And she reconstructed one, just like the ones at the ceremony. I realized then how much she'd been taking it all in.

MARIA: That's really powerful.

CECILY: Before we left the museum, Mia said goodbye to the objects and told them, "I hope you are able to get back to your original owners." She gets it, has an internal connectedness to our culture. I guess we're talking about those things together—the history, the exploitation, our need to reclaim ourselves. It's part of our conversations. Whereas with Vanessa—who's twelve—what I felt was that I didn't know how to give her a sense of what it means to be Filipina, because I didn't know. I was estranged from it; I don't speak the language, I can't cook the food. I've been immersed in whiteness all my life, and it taught me to be ashamed of being Filipina. What I conveyed in my early mothering was, "I don't know how to give you something that I don't have. And I'm mourning the loss of that."

MARIA: Even though you feel like you're still figuring out what being Filipina means to you, it's amazing that you've provided opportunities for your daughters to experience it with you. It's like you're a child in the process, too. You're taking it in, and integrating it for yourself, but you also are present for your daughters, witnessing how they receive it, too. And how they receive it will be different from how we internalize the experience, and meaningful in its own way. As we grow and evolve in our own decolonization process, we give them what we can. They may or may not "get it" as we would like them to. You are intentional about providing your daughters opportunities and the space to process those experiences. This inspires me to do the same in an active way. Identifying that it's important, and fighting for that time—this is the challenge, given the chaos of our lives as academics, mothers and Pinays. But to do it is healing. The fact that we're thinking about a summer camp with other Fil-Am families—creating these opportunities for ourselves—is empowering.

CECILY: What you said just now—providing our girls with as much as we can and having faith that they can make their own meaning, and integrate that into a whole sense of self—is making me realize that I need to work through my fear of raising daughters who will feel the emptiness, the alienation, that I've grappled with. Can I reframe it for myself, so my mothering isn't coming from a fear-based place? It comes back to that idea of believing we're good enough. We need to have enough trust in our mothering to know that our daughters will find their way, knowing it's not going to be perfect. I might need to start their therapy fund now [*shared laughter*].

MARIA: I wonder about how being Pinay plays out in Ella and Izzy's lives.

How do I teach them about the scars we inherit? As I seek healing with and within my community, will they also participate in this journey? Will they feel the need to heal? It's instinctual to project my own need for healing onto them. Are they not members of our community after all..are they not fully Pinay? I need to remind myself that *they are not me*. They are their own selves...growing, exploring, evolving. They need to ask their own questions about the world and who they are without me imposing.

CECILY: I struggle with that, with letting go.

MARIA: It's beautiful how you led Mia to the space at the museum, and she then internalized it and constructed her own space at home, to honor and embrace the sacred within her life. This act of *altar building* reminds me of how Ella and Izzy find connectedness and grounding on their own: respecting and blessing their titas and lolas, praying with family for the soul of a loved one who has passed, simple moments like making biko together in our kitchen. We make the rituals and the traditions sacred, and the act of doing this together is our ceremony. We may show them what an altar looks like for us and provide the ingredients, but they build them in their own ways. And then, *we learn* from their rich artistry. Perhaps there is good in letting go of struggling so hard to find our Filipina-ness and shaping that of our daughters. As we provide opportunities for our girls to experience who we are as Pinays, they do find their way and are enriched by it. Simultaneously, we are kinder to ourselves, and come to self-acceptance and peace about it.

Radically Loving Our Daughters, Ourselves, and Each Other: Our Reflections

MARIA: There are not many people with whom I can share the different parts of myself and the complexity in how they intersect...as a Pinay-mother, -scholar and educator, community activist, daughter, friend, spouse to a Jewish man raising two bi-racial, interfaith children together, ages five and nine. All of these identities have a special meaning to me. In my friendship with Cecily, I experience a warmth, authenticity and openness to receive and accept the many parts of who I am as a Pinay mother-scholar. Together we struggle with questions that are part of our ongoing decolonization: *How do we teach our children to honor their roots? What will we pass on? How do we sustain a sense of healing and self-acceptance in our mothering and in our work, as we negotiate a context of academia that can be demoralizing and dismissive of the endeavor to decolonize? How do we create a new, kinder paradigm that is cognizant of where we come from?* The act of sharing our vulnerability, experiencing together the discomfort and reward in pursuing these questions, and having someone to intimately engage in the discourse—this *pakikiisa*—has been healing to me.

Cecily: Writing this story with Maria has led me to an important distinction between *mother* and *mothering*: *mothering* is a verb. It's active, dynamic. *Mothering* provides a gracious space for me to confront my deepest fear—of failing my daughters. This fear is rooted in me not having had the opportunity, as an adult daughter, to resolve my conflicts with my mother and find answers to my questions about who she was, and therefore, who I am. Accepting the past, forgiving my parents, forgiving myself, and getting to a place of unconditional self-love, has been and continues to be a painful but transformational process. I believe that I can get beyond judgment and shame to a place of embracing and loving who I am and my own way of mothering. *Mothering* is a lifelong journey of constructing who I am—*unapologetically Pinay*—and sharing that with my daughters. Allyson Tintiangco-Cubales, in her theory of Pinayism, challenges us to (re)develop a Pinay sisterhood: how do we lift each other up when we've been taught to tear each other down? My relationship with Maria is a Pinayist space in which we define what it means for us to (re)love ourselves and each other.

---

[2] Tintiangco Cubales, A. (2005). Pinayism. In M. L. De Jesus (Ed.), *Pinay power: Theorizing the Filipina/American experience* (pp. 137-148). New York: Routledge.

Breaking Bones with My Mother

Karen Buenavista Hanna
Marlo Buenavista Hanna

My mother and I are connected. When I cry, her tears pour out through mine. We have broken our bones together. The bond between mother and child is magic.

"What is beautiful is broken." — Tala Khanmalek

In my darkest moments of pain, I have laid down crying on my bathroom floor. My friend commented how this was beautiful- how I intuitively knew that Mother Earth should hold me. I know that my pain is not only mine. It is the pain of my mother. And my father's mother. My dad said she died of a broken heart when he was just a small boy.

While pain can be beautiful, it can also be magic. Estela B., a healer and one of my dearest friends, feels intense headaches and nausea when physically near people and places with histories of trauma. An elder Mexicana healer explained that her sensitivity to energy leads her to feel other people's pain. Estela learned, "Feeling pain is good so we know what needs to be healed. But it's also important to know how to heal ourselves, otherwise we might absorb it and hurt our bodies." Knowing her experience is transformative. How might we see pain as an indicator of power rather than deficiency?

Illness can also be a symptom of magic. Unlike the Western view of illness as pathology, people throughout the world have thought about illness differently. For example, the Dagara people of Western Africa believe that mental disorders signal the birth of a healer. According to Malidoma

Patrice Somé, "Mental disorder, behavioral disorder of all kinds, signal the fact that two obviously incompatible energies have merged into the same field." They result when the person does not get assistance in dealing with the presence of the energy from the spirit realm. I wonder if physical illness might also be caused by the same energetic dissonances.

Deep down, our people know. My mother told me that there was a seruhano in our family. In my mom's region of Negros Occidental in the Philippines, seruhano are medicine men; one of many healers, miracle workers, and "see-ers." Their work carries on the pre-colonial legacy of Babaylan (also known as bailan, catooran, mamumuhat, diwatero, catalonan, babalian, alopogan, and dorarakit), who Ate Grace Nono describes as those who were respected in society as "priestesses/ritualists, healers/therapists, chanters/reciters of oral traditions, dancers, philosophers, [and] transmitters of culture" and connected to the spirit world (2013, 24). Tita Leny Strobel and Tita Lily Mendoza remind us that when the Spanish colonized the Philippines, most Babaylan were rounded up and murdered, many systematically fed to crocodiles (2013). They continue to exist today, still threatening to Christianity and the Spanish project of colonization."

Before he died, people visited my Tito Beboy's house so he could treat them for various sicknesses. His father, Lolo Caesar, my grandfather's brother, held all kinds of spiritual wisdom too. My mother also has a special sense. I hold this information close to my heart. I ask, what healing knowledge lies within my family's bloodline and in our spirits? What insight is waiting to be revealed?

My Mother's Broken Bones

Three years ago, my mother and I experienced severe physical changes within weeks of each other. She was living in Florida, while I was in Wisconsin and California.

It was on a hot day in August when my mother's leg snapped in half while she watered her plants. She lay for hours on the ground of her backyard in the thick humidity and sun. She hurled stones at the windows of the house to alert my father, who watched TV inside. When my dad finally found my mom, he couldn't lift her body. He called 911 and an ambulance arrived, rushing her to the emergency room.

We learned that my mother had experienced a spontaneous fracture of the largest bone in the body- the femur. It was the result of a medication she had ironically taken for 11 years to strengthen her bones. Neither the company nor her medical provider warned her that taking the medication for more than a couple of years could lead to such an outcome. Furthermore, an x-ray indicated a fracture in her other femur. The medication led her to acquire two broken legs- the second one ready to break at any moment.

As soon as I learned about my mom's fall, I called and heard her cry for the first time in my 32 years. When I flew to see her, vulnerability replaced her usual tough independent demeanor. She was filled with fear and anxiety. Hyper-vigilance arose over the smallest tasks, like leaving the house and taking a shower. Less than six months prior, my mother had retired from her 40+ year nursing career: employment that made her, like many other Filipinas, the breadwinner in our family. She had been the superwoman of our family. And now she was completely dependent on my dad and aunt to care for her.

My Joints and Bones

Two months after my mother's fracture, a week before my third year of my PhD program, I woke up with stiffness in my right hand. I could not clap at a conference I was attending. My feet were badly swollen and I had trouble walking up and down stairs. I was exhausted. Over a few weeks time, the pain spread to several other joints in my body. Soon I was wincing while getting out of bed.

I learned that I had rheumatoid arthritis (RA), a chronic progressive disease where the body's immune system shifts into overdrive, attacking its own joint tissue. After wearing down joint tissue, RA erodes the bones, leading to permanent deformity in as short as two years. Left untreated, inflammation can lead to complications in organs like the heart and lungs. When I was first diagnosed, my anti-CCP count, one marker of RA, was over 50 times the normal count. Already my elbows and middle finger have eroded and everyday they are puffy, tender, and warm to the touch.

The exact cause of RA remains unknown. Women are three times more likely than men to have RA, suggesting a possible gendered link between environmental stressors and RA. It is constant stress that I believe made me a strong candidate for RA. Maria Yellow Horse Brave Heart's work on trauma in Native American communities has shown that hyper-vigilance increases production of adrenaline and cortisol. Both are survival hormones related to "fight, flight, or freeze." Continuous production of these hormones can lead to major illness. Women of color in academia know we are likely to face one or more micro-aggressions a day. Our knowledge leads us to adopt a hyper-vigilant awareness to protect us from psychological harm. I believe I'd gotten so used to protecting myself in academia that my body's immune system, through the overproduction of survival hormones, literally locked into high gear.

My doctor and reiki practitioner both noticed something strangely co-incidental about the timing of my RA diagnosis and my mother's broken bones. "Something metaphysical," my doctor observed.

Unsent Letter to My Mother: May 2014

Dear Mom,
If I had the courage, I would call you everyday and tell you
how much pain I'm in.
How I limp when I walk
How I sometimes can't stand long enough to cook
How my body parts throb at night
How they wake me up in the middle of the night
And all I can think is: This must be how it feels to have been hit
by a truck.
I wish I could tell you how I can't leave the house sometimes
How I've laid on my bathroom floor crying
My baths my only solace
I wish I could pick up the phone to just to say hi,
To tell you I just cried in my professor's office
Because it took longer than usual to get there and I was late,

How I can't ride my bike today because I can't lean on the handlebars
How I haven't been to yoga in months because I can't do
downward dog
How I fear that one day I won't be able to carry my own baby.
But I also want to tell you all about what I'm doing to care for myself
How in the kitchen, I repeat to myself: "My food is my medicine"
You'd be proud, I hope, if I could just tell you everything.

But all I can say when we are on the phone are bits between
clenched teeth
And tense shoulders, to which you reply,
"Well don't lose weight. You need calcium. Where is your protein?"
To anyone else, I would admit
I'm nervous that I lost ten pounds in a month, but
I would reassure them that my nutritionist said I'm healthy.
That it was water weight and my weight will even out.
Without getting defensive, I would say, "Yes! I just did research on
vegetable-based protein." Or tell them, "I drink carrot juice everyday
for calcium."
I might say, "I'm not sure it will work, but I need to try."
But I can't tell you all these things because all I want to do is get off
the phone.
And you know it because you can hear it in my annoyed voice.
I think you wonder if I still love you.
And I feel terribly guilty.

But you see, I'm mad.
Months ago, I was real with you. You asked me how I was and I started
to cry. Why was I crying? I answered, "It's all so hard to deal with."
You told me to be strong. You said:
"Don't be weak. Don't be a crybaby. To get through this, you need to
fight or else it will get you."

But I think it's ok to cry, mom.
From a small age, I remember feeling so ashamed to cry in front of you

and everyone in our family.

"Karen, are you crying?" Phi Aom once asked, noticing me over the cereal box.

You all looked at me and smirked. I'm still really obvious when I cry.

My eyes fill up and turn glassy, hiding it makes it worse.

I still hide my tears from you.

I think I learned how to act "strong" from you.

It's interesting because I think you know- the more I "act" strong the more you know I don't feel strong. But it's a vicious cycle because I don't want to let you down. It doesn't make sense. It's funny how we do things and act in ways that we know don't make sense.

What I want from you mom, which I can't tell you now, but what I want

Is for you to be my mommy

To cradle me in your arms and let me cry to you

Even if we don't know what will happen to my body

Even if you don't agree with the choices I've made

Just tell me that you trust me. And tell me that everything will be ok.

Healing Tears

My parents flew to California to help me pack my apartment before a recent research trip. They scrubbed the windows and fixed my car. It was their vacation, and all they did was clean. They didn't complain once. As they were leaving, I started to cry. I cried so much.

My mom said, "Don't cry. It's bad luck." Defensively I replied, "You should cry, mom, tears are sacred, tears are healing."

They drove away and I cried and cried. I cried because I was grateful for their love and selflessness. I cried because I felt guilty for my short temper and impatience. I cried with worry, wondering if it would be the last time I'd ever see them- I am scared of losing them in their old age. But I also cried out of frustration that my mom would not listen to the sacred value of shedding tears. How they help us heal—scientifically and spiritually. I wished she would cry and not see it as wrong.

Letter to Me from My Mother: June 2016

Dear Kay,

I feel so bad I did not help you with your psychological, your laundry, etc.

I know I could not help you physically but I could have helped you with your stress.

The pain you feel, I feel it too.

I'm struggling my own self physically because of getting old and retirement and not being able to do things that I used to do when I was young because of my physical problems. I had surgery to my legs.

It coincided with your problems.

I had mine in July. You had yours in September.

So you reacted more, it was stress for you when hearing about my injury.

It may have had you have the disease because of stress on top of the stress you already have going to school. My feeling was the stress you had was all these things going on:

Your studies, your working, your things that you do in school,

Teaching on top of going to school and writing.

And stress being in the university and doing stuff that you're supposed to be doing because it's expected of you and all that stuff.

In other words,

It's the stress of life.

It's how you process yourself. If you internalize your stress something bad happens. If you defuse your stress and know how to handle it, you may be all right.

When you had it, the burden of the stress was on you.

You could not be there to help me do the stuff I should be doing- it added to the stress.

If this did not happen to me would it happen to you? We don't know.

Mine is more of a physical thing that happened because it was a chemical reaction to my body that I took for a long time.

You had nothing to do with what I had.

But I feel that what happened to you was because of what happened to me. The hair that broke the camel's back- yeah the hair weighs nothing, but because the camel is already strained, any amount of pressure broke it.

So the moral of the story is: You have to defuse your stress in a way you have an outlet for it.

Don't internalize your problems. It's what I normally do.

What you think of yourself, what can you do about it? If you can't do anything about it—you deal with it and get the stress out of your system. Go see a movie, listen to music, you don't think about your problems.

"'My mother and I work to unravel the knot.' This is how theory develops,"
—Aurora Levins Morales, Cherríe Moraga, and Gloria Anzaldúa

I have been conducting oral histories of activists. How is it that I know so much more about strangers than my own family? Reflecting on this, I interviewed both of my parents recently and recorded stories of them remembering their lives. As we sat together at our kitchen table, I asked my mother why she doesn't cry. I was stunned.

She said, "I do cry, but I just don't let anyone see." She explained that when she got ready to move to the US, her brother, Edwin, gave her $200. It was a lot of money he had saved, especially in 1970. My mom and Tito Edwin were very close. When they hugged goodbye, he cried. To my mother, it was funny. Here was this big tough guy crying. "Why are you crying?" she teased. "I'll be back soon."

Tito Edwin died before my mother returned to the Philippines to visit. That is why she says it's bad luck to cry.

"The pain you feel, I feel it too…. I feel that what happened to you is because of what happened to me."

I feel in my heart that when I cry, I cry my mother's tears too. I cry the tears that my mother lets no one see. And perhaps I also cry the tears of both my grandmothers and their mothers too.

My mother reminds me that things are not what they seem. We may think we understand someone, but we know much less than we actually do.

My journey with my mother teaches me that sometimes our pain and tears are the result of experiences that reach beyond our own lifetimes and geographies. But she also teaches me that we already have the wisdom we need to survive and heal. Together, we learn that it is the stories we uncover that offer us confidence to seek out this wisdom and understand our lives and each other better. What stories are waiting to be told? I'm still asking.

She

mgb

i.

In this place, She is nothing. She is furniture. She looks around to see a few other faces that look like hers; slanted eyes, dark hair, broad noses, but they are furniture also. She continues to scribble down notes on her college rule paper and counts the minutes left in class. She walks through the campus, sidestepping the slower pace folks, avoiding petitions and dodging skaters. She keeps her head down and eyes forward. A white student shoves a homemade flier in her face.

"Happy Womyn's Day!"

She looks at the paper. The women's symbol is drawn in crayon.

"Thank you." she says and hurriedly walks away.

In the Quad she can hear a voice on the bullhorn. The language reminds her of home and she turns towards the voice. She follows her ears until she is looking at a stage full of women. Another woman grabs the mic.

"Thank you sister. I'd like to thank all our beautiful sisters out there listening today. If you just joining us, I'd like to welcome you to our women's rally. Today is a day that our voices will be heard! Now I'd like to introduce to you three talented beautiful strong women. Give it up for Jennifer, Ashley and Sarah!"

The first took the mic and began.

"He saw her and began a seven year cha cha with a woman who would not give him the time of day. This was not allowed. She, a white woman and he, a not white man. Through their love a girl was introduced to the world as a demon child, a freak of nature. She walked a path in which she was convinced that she should question who she is, who she loves more and that she was not good enough for either side. Though she was

American, she was treated less. The law had no place for her. She was an other. She educated herself, talked to other hapas like herself and found her voice behind a bullhorn. She will never again allow anyone else make her question anything in her life."

The next woman took the mic.

"I was once a goddess walking the earth. I ruled side by side with men and we were equal. I once was a healer, a counselor, a priestess. I was a goddess on earth. Then they came and made themselves kings and gods. Said we were not good enough, not clean enough, not civil enough. For 300 years they beat us into thinking that. For another hundred years we were told we were good enough. Just not for their women, their jobs, their education. We were allowed to make a new home in a new land, and then asked to go back. They made their home in our land and used our goods, our women, our labor, for themselves. Then they needed us again. Took all our smart ones and made false promises again. To this day, I am still a goddess, a healer, a counselor. I am nurse, a teacher, a mother, a daughter, a sister, a friend."

She walks away before the next woman grabs the mic, trying to process what she just heard. She stares out from the crowd and misses her train. When She reaches her small apartment, She sits down in front of a mirror and calls her mother.

"Tell me what it was like where you are from."

"We have no land. We are nomads. When the war came we floated across the river in tires and prayed not to drown. We went from mountain to mountain always trying to be quicker than the soldiers. We saw so many bad things. America said they would take care of us. They said they would help us. But when we came they had no room, no jobs. Nobody want- ed us here. There were others that went blind. No one knew what was wrong. When we looked for work, we took whatever they would give us. It was so different from home, now we could be whatever we want because we were in America. Now we could be making more money than the men."

"Mama, was it hard? I mean I know it was hard, but did you ever think you wouldn't make it?

"I was never allowed to think I was broken."

ii.

Mama

I know I never show it, but I do appreciate you. I didn't realize until recently how much of yourself you sacrificed for us, for me. It must have been a surprise, knowing that you were pregnant at 40. Even bigger surprise that I wasn't the boy you wanted. Was it hard to start over as a parent? Was it harder to start a new life in the states? I remember going with you to work, or your works. I remember the daycare where I forgot Tagalog and learned Spanish. I remember playing Nintendo for hours in the Kmart electronics section, while you worked at the check outs. I remember you tucking me in and you going to make carpets. Yet when I woke up you made sure that breakfast was on the table and lunch was on the counter. When papa finished his 12 hour day you were still at work. I remember on Friday nights when you would get paid and even though it was late you went grocery shopping and would send your whole check on next week's food. I know now, that you did what was expected of you. What you were suppose to do as a wife and mother? Did you ever get mad that you never really saw us? That you had to work all the time while my friends' mothers stayed home or went on vacations. Were you disappointed in us when we didn't do our best or get in trouble? What is it like, mama, to be you?

W. Kyle De Ocera

How to make home

It's simple: do whatever it takes.
It's simple: do whatever it takes.
It's simple: do whatever it takes.
It's simple: do whatever it takes.
It's simple: do whatever it takes.
It's simple: do whatever it takes.
It's simple: do whatever it takes.
It's simple: do whatever it takes.
It's simple: do whatever it takes.
It's simple: do whatever it takes.
It's simple: do whatever it takes.
It's simple: do whatever it takes.
It's simple: do whatever it takes.
It's simple: do whatever it takes.
It's simple: do whatever it takes.
It's simple: do whatever it takes.
It's simple: do whatever it takes.
It's simple: do whatever it takes.

THE PILIPINX RADICAL
IMAGINATION
READER
BIOS

Editors

DR. MELISSA-ANN NIEVERA-LOZANO
...sees storytelling as medicine. Born and bred in southeast San Diego, CA, she is the child of Filipino (Igorot and Waray) immigrants. Her research sources from women-of-color radical thought, which guides her community work surrounding the intersectional struggles of racism, classism, and heteropatriarchy impacting our lives across families and generations. Melissa currently resides in San Jose, CA where she is raising two little boys, Mateo and Dante, with her partner Dennis, while teaching ethnic studies courses throughout the Bay Area.

ANTHONY (TONY) ABULENCIA SANTA ANA
...is a doctoral candidate in the International/Multicultural Education department at the University of San Francisco and identifies as a HELLA Bay Area Pin@y, born in San Francisco and raised in San Jose, CA. He globe trots mother earth seeking and searching to find truth and beauty in our ever-changing vast world. Tony's passions are creatively expressing himself through music, movement, words and basketball. He always lives his life to the fullest so he hopes to inspire others to do the same.

Contributors

YSHMAEL "YSH" CABANA
...is a Philippine-born, Canada-based a cultural worker and educator. He had designs exhibited in Manila, New York and San Francisco for resilient school after 2013's typhoon Haiyan occurrence which then prompted him to write his poem he contributed in this volume. He is one of the founding members of Filipino-Canadian Writers and Journalists Network, and is active in community organizing with Pilipinx youth group Anakbayan-Toronto.

CAROLINE CALDERON
...was born and raised in Los Angeles but also calls the Bay home. She gives much love and gratitude to the spaces and people that have also raised her: Veterans Equity Center, Pin@y Educational Partnerships, Bindlestiff Studio, Urban X Indigenous, Migrante SOMA/TL and SOMA Pilipinas. Thank you to Ntozake Shange, who wrote "for colored girls who have considered suicide / when the rainbow is enuf"—your play has helped me in the darkest of times.

ADAM RABUY CRAYNE
...divides home between the East Bay Area of California and the National Capital Region of the Philippines. A former Philippine public school teacher, he now works for a public relations firm on projects that promote peace, culture, and sustainability. His work has been featured in publications by the UCSD Cross Cultural Center, the Center for Art and Thought (CA+T), and Create Fam Studio.

Dr. Roderick Daus-Magbual

...is the Director of Program Development for Pin@y Educational Partnerships (PEP), a social justice education leadership pipeline that utilizes Filipina/o American Studies to serve students K-College students. He is also an instructor at Skyline College in San Bruno, CA where he teaches in both the Kababayan and CIPHER Learning Communities.

Dr. Arlene Daus-Magbual

...is the Director for the Asian American and Pacific Islander Student Services at San Francisco State University (SFSU) and the Organizational Director of Pin@y Educational Partnerships (PEP). She has taught at University of San Francisco School of Education and SFSU Asian American Studies Department and Education Minor Program.

W.Kyle De Ocera

...is an artist and educator born in Project 8, Quezon City, Philippines. He received his Bachelor of Arts in Creative Writing at San Francisco State University and Master of Fine Arts in Creative Writing at Long Island University. He currently teaches in the South Bay Area.

Dominique Defoe

...is a blackipina college student living in Colorado. Her favorite class is world history and she loves reading, the color red, and chai tea lattes.

Maharaj "Raju" Desai

...is a PhD candidate in Education at UH Mānoa. He teaches language and culture courses with the Filipino program at UH Mānoa and is also adjunct faculty in Philippine Studies at City College of San Francisco. He received his BA and MA in Asian American Studies from San Francisco State University.

Bernard Ellorin, PhD.

...is an adjunct faculty in the Arts & Humanities Department at Miramar College in San Diego, California. He received his PhD in Ethnomusicology from the University of Hawai'i at Manoa in 2015. Ellorin's academic and community work spans over 26 years educating Filipino American communities and non-Filipino American communities in Los Angeles, San Jose, Michigan, San Diego, California and Honolulu, Hawaii on Philippine music and Filipino diasporic performing arts.

Trinidad Escobar

...is a full-time artist, writer, mother, and educator. Her work explores the spirit and its manifestations as connective tissue between sisterhood, queer relationships, and nature. She lives in Oakland with her son.

Lani Paguio Felicitas

...is a grassroots organizer with Anakbayan Portland and an iskolar ng bayan from Lewis & Clark College. She navigates the classroom and the streets, linking the personal to the political, connecting the diaspora to her mother's land, putting anthropology into practice. She encourages all oppressed peoples, whether or not they have gone to school, to lean into their struggles and to wage a fight for their liberation.

MARIA JOY FERRERA
…is a second-generation Pinay and faculty member at DePaul University in Chicago. Her areas of education, research and activism revolve around community-based, socially just decolonizing methodologies and practices; the impact of historical trauma on ethnic identity development; and mental health and health disparities within minority and immigrant communities. She continues to find joy in the evolving richness of multi-ethnic, interfaith family life with her husband, Adam, and their two daughters, Ella and Isabel.

NICOLE GERVACIO
…is an interdisciplinary artist based in Oakland, California–Occupied Huichin. Inspired by genealogy, the body, and memory she explores themes of identity, destruction and deterioration, permanence versus impermanence, and intersectionality. Her work is driven by the fear of forgetting.

PATRICIA "TRISH" GUEVARRA
…is a 2nd generation Pinay of Kapampangan and Batangueña roots. She currently lives in the Bay Area, CA where she's a social justice college educator/counselor.

MARYCARL GUIAO
…is a daughter of the Maharlikan diaspora, engaged in deepening understanding of critical consciousness and precolonial cultural regeneration. After years of bottom-up community organizing (incl producing Migrant Matters Radio for campus/community radio, co-founding Chonnonton Territory-based migrant worker advocacy collective Fuerza/Puwersa), she arrives in the formal interarts world continuing to honor persxnal and collective lived realities, and to support acts that nurture: who We all are, Her/Their/OurStories, and all of Our ancestral cultures where respecting nature is central. As a spoken word artist and a student of Obo Manobo kulintang music, through performance that melds the two art forms, she aims to both: communicate an appreciation for sounds associated with cultures where building healthy relationships with all life is priority, and spread awareness about interpersonal and wider relations/systems of abuse, incl the struggles of Indigenous peoples living at the foot of Mt Apo.

KAREN BUENAVISTA HANNA
…is a PhD Candidate in the Department of Feminist Studies at the University of California, Santa Barbara, a Mellon/ACLS Dissertation Completion Fellow, and Woodrow Wilson Women's Studies Dissertation Fellow. For almost a decade prior to her PhD program, Karen was a New York City Public School Teacher, pre-GED teacher at the Brooklyn Public Library, and community organizer who worked alongside Filipina/o immigrant youth and domestic workers. Her writing has been published in *Hyphen Magazine*, *Hypatia: A Journal of Feminist Philosophy*, and is forthcoming in *Frontiers: A Journal of Women Studies*.

MARLO BUENAVISTA HANNA
…is a happy retired registered nurse who lives with her husband in Flagler Beach, Florida. She was a critical care nurse, and in her forty-five years of nursing, she has worked in the ICU, PACU, Emergency Department, Cardiac Cath Lab, Cancer, Dialysis, Pediatric, and

Medical Surgical Units. Presently, Marlo enjoys fishing and doing volunteer work for Flagler County Volunteer Services.

CECILY RELUCIO HENSLER
...is an educator in Chicago focused on developing current and future educators of Color to become culturally and community responsive leaders. Through her research, teaching, and organizing, Cecily is committed to struggling for the radical healing, humanization and self-determination of educators of Color, as one component of the larger political struggle to decolonize U.S. schooling of youth of Color in urban spaces. While her identity and experiences as an educator are central to who she is, Cecily's most cherished, important and challenging role in life is mothering her two Pinay and white daughters, Vanessa and Mia, ages 14 and 10.

TERESA HODGES
...with a BA/Ethnic Studies, an MA/Asian American Studies, and a PhD Student/Educational Foundations, has been studying/organizing about mixed race since 2000. She works to delve deeper in the relationship between mixed race and Blackness and Filipina/o/x-ness and in larger discussions of equity and race in society.

JULIA HOLT
...believes that if you are kind to the world, the world is kind to you, however, it may not always be kind back. I believe if you persevere through the hard times, you build a strong will within yourself, realizing that you can do and conquer anything. I, Julia Holt, believe that I am strong, but I will be stronger.

JANNA AÑONUEVO LANGHOLZ
...is an interdisciplinary artist born and based in St. Louis, Missouri. Her work explores her identity as a second-generation Filipino American and relationship to place through photography, installations, performances, and participatory projects. She is the founder and editor of Filipino American Artist Directory, an initiative to connect and promote Fil/Am artists across the U.S. and beyond.

KEITH RAYOS LARA
...is a community college student hoping to be a lawyer in the future. His interests include attending stage plays and reading folklore. His goal after graduate school is to be actively involved in community activism particularly in the Pilipinx sphere.

KIRIN AMILING MACAPUGAY
...is an assistant professor at San Diego City College. She serves on the City of San Diego Commission for Arts and Culture and was former Commissioner for the California Commission on Asian and Pacific Islander American Affairs as an appointee of Governor Brown. In January of 2017, she was honored as a "Present Day Civil Rights Woman Leader" by RISE San Diego. Kirin founded Asian Pacific Islander Community Actions (APICA) to serve as a nonprofit hub for grassroots projects including the Paradise Hills Night Market, FilAmFest/Barangay Cultural Arts Movement, and the Kuya Ate Mentorship Program.

mgb

…has been a poet since she first learned how to write her name, an educator since 2006, & a wannabe dramaturg since spring 2016. Born on one of the seven thousand islands of the Philippine Arkipelago, she was raised in the dusty town of Porterville CA & now lives in San Francisco, less than a mile away from the beach. Her publications include *Tayo Literary Magazine*, *The Operating System*, & can be seen on stage at Bindlestiff Studios.

PELE PAGASA

Read Emmanuel Lacaba's "An Open Letter to Filipino Artists." End Martial Law in Mindanao! STR.

JULIUS PARAS

…has advocated for the voice and expression of Filipinos from his college days at Stanford University to his roles as social entrepreneur and technology startup executive in the Philippines. Julius is a champion of kindness, compassion, and the courage to be both. He is grateful for his life journey and the many lessons learned along the way.

OSCAR PEÑARANDA

…was born in Barugo, Leyte, Philippines, then moved to Manila at five years of age, then away to America (Canada then U.S.) at 12 years old. As an educator, writer, and coordinator of events and workshops, as well as travel guide to the Philippines. One of the founders of the birth of Ethnic Studies while at San Francisco State University. Recipient of the most prestigious award Gawad ng Alagad ni Balagtas, for lifetime achievements, by the Writers Guild of the Philippines (UMPIL).

REV. JOSEPH ALLEN RUANTO-RAMIREZ

…is a Katutubo American (father–Yloko & Ipugoo, mother–Hambali, Ita, & Iranun) and a refugee from the the Philippines who came to the United States in 1991 because of the eruption of Mt. Pinatubo (Apu Namalyari). He is a PhD student in Cultural Studies at Claremont Graduate University focusing on Katutubo diasporic identities in Philippine-America. His primary research question is — "What happens when the Igorot & Moro tells the Filipinx that what the Filipinx is performing is not real?"

JANICE LOBO SAPIGAO

…is the author of two books of poetry: *Like a Solid to a Shadow* (Timeless, Infinite Light, 2017) and *microchips for millions* (Philippine American Writers and Artists, Inc., 2016) and three other chapbooks. She was one of KQED Arts' 2017 Women to Watch, a VONA/ Voices and Kundiman Fellow, and the Associate Editor of *TAYO Literary Magazine*. She co-founded Sunday Jump open mic in L.A. and earned her M.F.A. in Writing from CalArts, and she has a B.A. in Ethnic Studies with Honors from UC San Diego.

LEAH K. SICAT

…is a second-generation Filipina American and transnational feminist residing in the Bay Area, CA. Her work—informed by her educational and organizing experiences in California, New York, and South Korea—aims to center and uplift the voices of women of color.

EILEEN R. TABIOS
...loves books and has released over 50 collections of poetry, fiction, essays, and experimental biographies from publishers in nine countries and cyberspace. Her writing and editing works have received recognition through awards, grants and residencies. More information is available at http://eileenrtabios.com

DR. ALLYSON TINTIANGCO-CUBALES
...is a professor in the College of Ethnic Studies at San Francisco State University. She is also the founder and director of teacher development of Pin@y Educational Partnerships. She is also one of the co-director of Teaching Excellence Network and Community Responsive Education.

MAHALAYA TINTIANGCO-CUBALES
...(12 years old when this was written) is a Pinay who loves to move. She dances classical and contemporary ballet, modern, jazz, and hip hop 7 days a week at the Westlake School for the Performing Arts. In 2016-2017, she was named by New York City Dance Alliance as the National Junior Outstanding Dancer and in 2018, she received the Youth America Grand Prix Award in San Francisco.

JONATHAN AREOLA VALDEZ
...was born and raised in San Diego, CA. He is currently working on his PhD at the University of Hawai'i at Mānoa in the department of American Studies. Jonathan is a self-trained cook, wine and beer maker, and bartender.

SALVADOR VELASCO
...comes from Bicol & Masbate, Philippines; rooting in Paradise Hills, San Diego, CA. The voice, vision, passion and hard work of the Pinxy spirit is alive and international. It's an honor.

KAREN MARIE MALIWAT VILLA
...is a queer, diasporic Pinay born and raised in Oxnard, California. Her family is Capampañgan and Ilocano of the provinces San Miguel, Tarlac and Victoria, Laguna in the Philippines. Karen is an ethnographer, professor and social activist, and has directed *Visibilizing Queer Pinays in Southern California*, a collaborative film series of ethnographic shorts on queer Pinay inner resilience, resourcefulness, responsibility, and re/creation. Twitter: @PinayDiaspora.

DR. LILY ANN BOLO VILLARAZA
...currently serves as the Department Chair of the Philippine Studies Department at the City College of San Francisco. She recently completed her PhD in History, with a specialization in Southeast Asia, from Northern Illinois University.

ROVIELLE YAMAKI
R. Yamaki's life choices have redefined that sometimes "home" could just really be where the grass grows greener. Today, with her husband Kentaro and their beautiful daughter Cocomi Elle, they thrive in a chosen reality where diversity is celebrated.

Philippine American Writers and Artists, Inc.

P.O. Box 31928
San Francisco, California
94131-0928
www.pawainc.com • pawa@pawainc.com

SELECTIONS: READING FOR THE YOUNG AND OLD
edited by Penélope V. Flores (2002)

WHISPER OF THE BAMBOO:
An anthology of Philippine American Writers and Artists
edited by Penélope V. Flores, Allen Gaborro (2004)

FIELD OF MIRRORS:
An anthology of Philippine American Writers and Artists
edited by Edwin A. Lozada (2008)

THE PHILIPPINE JEEPNEY: A FILIPINO FAMILY METAPHOR
Understanding the Filipino American Family
by Penélope V. Flores with Araceli N. Resus (2008)

GOOD-BYE VIENTIANE: UNTOLD STORIES OF FILIPINOS IN LAOS
by Penélope V. Flores (2005, 2010)

REMEMBERING RIZAL: VOICES FROM THE DIASPORA
A collection of pieces by Rizal and writers inspired by Rizal
edited by Edwin A. Lozada (2011)

THE FIRE BENEATH: TALES OF GOLD
by Almira Astudillo Gilles (2012)

TO LOVE AS ASWANG: SONGS, FRAGMENTS, AND FOUND OBJECTS
by Barbara Jane Reyes (2015)

FLIPS 2015
A Filipino American Anthology, A Reprint
edited by Serafin Syquia, Bayani Mariano
Introduction by Juanita Tamayo Lott (2015)

microchips for millions
by Janice L. Sapigao (2016)